THE
BLACK CLOUD

within me

BY

KEITH HORTON

TRAFFORD

USA ▪ Canada ▪ UK ▪ Ireland

Cover illustration by Karin Huggens and Type treatment by Zenon Slawinski
Editor–Melanie Rigney

Note for Librarians: A cataloguing record for this book is available from Library
and Archives Canada at www.collectionscanada.ca/amicus/index-e.html
ISBN 1-4251-0545-9

Offices in Canada, USA, Ireland and UK

Book sales for North America and international:
Trafford Publishing, 6E–2333 Government St.,
Victoria, BC V8T 4P4 CANADA
phone 250 383 6864 (toll-free 1 888 232 4444)
fax 250 383 6804; email to orders@trafford.com
Book sales in Europe:
Trafford Publishing (UK) Limited, 9 Park End Street, 2nd Floor
Oxford, UK OX1 1HH UNITED KINGDOM
phone +44 (0)1865 722 113 (local rate 0845 230 9601)
facsimile +44 (0)1865 722 868; info.uk@trafford.com
Order online at:
trafford.com/06-2303

10 9 8 7 6 5 4 3

Table of Contents

Prelude

"Adapt yourself to the things among which your lot has been cast and love sincerely the fellow creatures with whom destiny has ordained that you shall live." Marcus Aurelius

I AM THE LUCKIEST man in the world.

I'm blessed to live in this great country and blessed to have a wonderful family, friends, and acquaintances. I'm fortunate to have been on this earth for over forty years with its ups and downs and survive thus far with sound mind and able body. I'm blessed to have attended a historically black college or university (HBCU) and afterwards to have spent twenty years protecting the freedom of this great nation. I'm blessed to be part of organizations that really care about the future, our youth. I'm lucky to have been in the presence of positive men and women who may not be giants in the sight of many, but who are supermen and superwomen from my viewpoint. I'm thankful and grateful for those before me who sacrificed and even gave their lives to ensure that I can do the things that they could only dream of. I'm blessed to have had people believe in me, push me, and even give me a second chance. I'm blessed to see and notice the wonderful things of this world and stare in awe as I know there has to be a higher power.

But there is a cloud within me that has reached its saturation point and what precipitates is not water but showers of words. The color of my cloud is black, because it has been in the shadow of other clouds. This cloud of mine is about to come out of the shadows and pour out its contents to rain on some but hopefully to stimulate and energize others thoughts. Did I tell you how blessed I am? I would like to thank you for picking up my book and blessing me with your valuable time. I wanted to say these things up front because as you read, you may think I'm another angry black man. I'm not; just passionate about my views.

I'm writing this book as a way of expressing my feelings and thoughts. I'm not an expert in any of these topics; however, I always wanted to form my viewpoints into reading material for others to accept or reject. I'm just an ordinary person who always had pent-up emotions, but didn't have a platform to speak my two cents. Hopefully, this book expresses some of the concerns of the average man because that is exactly where/what I am... average.

I guess you can say that I'm fed up with the so-called black leaders who try to tell us that the government is the answer to as well as the fault of all of our problems. I'm fed up with the soft-spoken ministers and preachers who are too afraid of speaking the truth about the rampant problems in our culture, and I'm fed up with the lack of vision on their part to see that the church is more than a meeting place on Sunday to collect their salaries. I'm fed up with some of the influential blacks who pontificate and do absolutely nothing else to help the plight of other blacks and minorities. I'm fed up with the mind-sets of some folks who view themselves as victims no matter what the circumstance... it's always some else's fault. And I'm fed up with the hypocrisy in the political parties. Yes, I'm fed up, but I'm also encouraged by the promise of many of our youth and encouraged by the wonderful things average people are doing to make a difference in the world.

I wanted to give you an opportunity to know a little about me, and from there we will jump into a series of topics that may be controversial and sensitive but hopefully thought provoking. I've always been a very observant person; maybe something I say in this book will make you go hmmm!!

Chapter I

Laying Bare the Heart

"What lies behind us and what lies ahead of us are tiny matters compared to what lives within us." Anonymous

Life Lesson I: "There will come a time when you need to defend yourself."

I GREW UP in a small town in southwest Georgia, the parents of schoolteachers. I would say that I had a privileged upbringing in the sense that I had two loving parents who believed in fairness, discipline, hard work, and kindness and who had strong religious beliefs. My mother is a strong-willed, opinionated woman; I probably received those genes. She is also a very kind human being who will do almost anything for anyone. My father was a strong man, dark, handsome, a great dresser with a resonate, deep bass voice.

I grew up as an only child in a stable home with parents who did not spoil me. My parents weren't from big families and we didn't have the large family reunions that so many

11

other black families did. I had only a few cousins, and we were not close due to distance. My parents showered me with love, but I still missed that relationship with family members my own age.

We lived in the so-called country, not really the country but definitely not the suburbs. We lived in a trailer on an acre-and-a-half plot of ground bounded by dirt roads. Across the street, our neighbors lived in an old, dilapidated home with no running water. The kids took baths in a washtub on top of one of the many broken-down cars that littered the front and back yards. For fun, our neighbors would let a pig loose and then chase him down. My mother objected to my playing with them on a regular basis… do you suppose we thought we were better?

One hot summer day. The kids across the street and I were playing a game and we began to argue. Before I knew it, one the boys knocked the living daylights out of me. I buckled over and began to cry and then I beat a path straight to the trailer. My father asked me what happened and I told him the boy across the street hit me. Now, I thought to myself that my father would confront the boy's father and go and defend me… how wrong I was. My father looked at me, took his belt off, and commenced to whipping my tail for not defending myself.

Life Lesson II: "Unfortunately, racism is a fact of life, learn how to deal with it."

My mother and a few other black women taught at a predominately white school during the late sixties and early seventies. Busing was not in full force as of yet but the integration of teachers was slowly trickling in.

Since I wasn't performing to her expectations at the local school, she took me out of that school and enrolled me in hers so that she could watch over my teachers and my academic progress. I was enrolled into a school with only six blacks, and another black and I were in the second grade.

I thought I assimilated well; I played with all of the kids, learned their music, and learned their slang/talk. I guess at seven or eight, you just don't have the ability to see through people's real intentions; everything and everyone are innocent until proven otherwise. I was about to experience something that would change the way I thought about people and my outlook on folks.

I was doing OK in all of my classes except one and my mother, who had been the hawk of the six black kids in the school, swooped down to see why I was doing so poorly there. Having parents who are interested in your education can take a child a long way in life. My mother asked me where my book was for that class, and I stated that I did not receive a book for that subject. All hell was about to break loose; everyone in my class had been issued a book except me. My mother confronted the teacher, and she admitted that she did not give me a book. I don't know what was going through that teacher's mind; maybe she couldn't accept the fact that she had to teach a black boy, but whatever it was it haunted her for years to come. She apologized to my mother and continued to apologize years after that incident until her death. We forgave her, but never forget about that incident.

At my twenty-year high school class reunion, I was approached by one of my elementary classmates who said he wanted to apologize for something he said when we were in second grade. He was obviously intoxicated and at this particular point in my life, I didn't really want to hear what he called me. So, I told him that whatever he said or did, I forgave him, said that was the past and let's keep it in the past. The alcohol got the best of him and he exclaimed, "I called you a nigger when we were in second grade." He even had the audacity to say it again: "That's right, Keith, I called you a nigger and I'm sorry." He went on to say that he had been looking for me since I finished college and was tracking my progress through the Army and wanted to apologize, so much that when he saw me he had to confront me with this information. I accepted his apology, we hugged, and I wished him the best of luck in all of his future endeavors. I would encounter many other overt instances of racism, but learned how to deal with them because of the life lesson taught to me in grade school.

Life Lesson III: "There is always someone worse off than you."

I matriculated through elementary school learning a new culture, only keeping in touch with my roots through the church and sports.

My mother thought it important to get me around the people who were the movers and shakers in small-town Albany, Georgia, so I belonged to the YMCA and Jack and Jill organization. (Jack and Jill was a mentorship program focusing on character development and leadership). Back in the day, most blacks were relegated to the Boys/Girls Club because of the inordinate costs to gain membership in the YMCA. I fit in well at the Y since I had some athletic ability, but didn't think I was truly accepted into Jack and Jill, maybe because my parents were only teachers and maybe because I wasn't the most handsome boy around.

During a typical week, I went to Sunday morning Bible school, Sunday morning worship, Sunday night worship, Wednesday night Bible school, and Thursday night song practice. I did chores at the church on Saturday if I didn't have a sports event. Sundays were the best. I got a chance to emulate my daddy by dressing sharp, and heard the minister preach fire and brimstone every Sunday. After service, if my mother didn't cook collards and chicken, then we were off to our favorite restaurant to eat collards, chicken, potato soufflé, pork rinds, biscuits, cornbread, peach cobbler, and good ole Southern tea, the kind that will give you diabetes if you drink the whole pitcher. I didn't know what a doggy bag was, but I knew about that white napkin filled with chicken and biscuits going into my mother's pocketbook. Heck, after we ate that feast, it was a task to get home even though we only lived a few miles away. I swear my parents had to keep each other awake to make it home.

When we got home, my father and I would dash to the sofa to see who got sleeping rights while watching TV. After my mother woke up from her nap, she would wake us up and remind us that it was a sin to stay home and not attend Sunday night worship, so off we would go to men's and women's training class before worship. After part II of fire and brimstone, it would be snack time and that consisted of the best hot dogs around and a dozen Krispy Kreme doughnuts.

During my adolescent years I excelled in athletics, and that along with church kept me away from the evil so many young people get caught up in. On certain Sunday nights before our snack, we would visit the sick and shut-ins. We would go by the house of a paraplegic woman, was paralyzed from her neck down, to offer communion. Every time we entered, she would have this beautiful smile on her face and never complained about anything in her life. She would always ask you how you are doing and wanted to know what was going on in your life. Before you entered the room, you might have thought what you were going to say to encourage her but by the time you left, she would have given you the encouragement and inspiration to do your best during that week. She was truly a Godsend.

Life Lesson IV: "Discipline is required to be consistently successful."

Through my junior high years, I had two very strong men as coaches and mentors. Both men wanted me to excel on the field or court as well as in life.

During football and basketball practice, we would get the living daylights knocked out of us if we didn't follow instructions or failed to execute the plays as Coach drew them up. He would out of nowhere would hit you with a Mike Tyson-like jab straight to the breastbone, and you better not cry, ball them fists up, poke a lip out, or mutter under your breath. The only correct response was, "Coach, I'll get it right the next time."

If you screwed up during the basketball game, Coach would take you out of the game. Before you sat down he would do one of two things: punch you in the chest in front of everyone, including the referees, fans, principal, and parents, or pinch you on the arm, side, or wherever flesh was available and while doing so tell you how jacked up you were out on the court. We all knew Coach meant the best for us; the fans in the stands knew Coach took this thing seriously; parents knew Coach was an extension of them; and our peers respected the players for their toughness, humility, and emotional and mental capacity to be reprimanded in public.

During my adolescence, we moved into the suburbs, a nice neighborhood, blacks and whites living side by side. That lasted only a short time; soon, the complexion of the neighborhood changed to an all-black neighborhood. To this day, I have never understood white flight.

I continued to play football in high school, and when I was a sophomore and a junior, we lost every football game. We played in one of the toughest regions in the nation (Valdosta and Lowndes High were nationally ranked), and it showed during those two years as we were beat by thirty or more points by almost every team in the region. It was so bad that during one halftime, our opponents stayed on the field, drank sodas, and watched the halftime show; they were beating us 42-0 at half. Everyone told me I should quit. Coach told us that we would win one day and I, along with many other players, believed in him. During the off-season before my last year, we busted our butts in the weight room and on the field to improve. That next year, we went 6-4 and made it to the playoffs, beating one of the nationally ranked teams who humiliated us the previous year. That was a rewarding year because we saw the fruits of our labor and it demonstrated that when you apply yourself, hard work pays off. We also learned another lesson during that season, which was restraint and dignity. Even though teams embarrassed us previously, when we were in a position to do the same to them, our coach chose to take the high road and we ensured we won but kept the game respectable.

Life Lesson V: "Don't expect to receive something just because you did ok and if you want something don't rely on others to make it happen."

During my junior and senior years, I had my real first girlfriend. I will never forget when my mother told me, "You better treat that girl like you would want your sister to be treated." She did not just say it in passing; she elaborated on it until I got the point. She was saying, "You are about to engage with one of God's most precious gifts—a woman. Therefore, treat her with respect and kindness." I did, and have never forgotten that talk. Women are the key to existence; therefore, treat them as such.

Throughout my high school years, I experienced tragedy. Two friends were killed in car accidents; one was sixteen and the other, seventeen. Everyone will experience death of a friend or loved one at some point in their life; however, it's hard on a young person to endure these types of experiences.

The current generation probably experiences even more of these tragedies due to the increased violence in our society. A kid nowadays has to be careful of what he or she says, because anything that could be perceived as a threat to another kid could mean death. No longer can our kids fight it out fair and square. Heck, they don't even know how to fight. The only thing they know who to do is to pick up a gun or knife to permanently injure or kill someone. Do you remember back in the day when kids were able to resolve their differences? When the teacher broke up a fight prematurely and the two combatants didn't have the chance to settle their differences, the other kids would pass the word that the fight would be finished after school. Then, behind the school or at a park, the kids would form a circle so that the two could duke it out on fair terms. Each fighter had a person or agent who would ensure there was no foul play—straight-up fighting, no guns, no knives, no gangs jumping on one person. It was you against one other person. (Better yet, do you remember Coach getting the two fighters together in the gym and outfitting them with gloves and letting them duke it out for all to see until they were completely exhausted?) The two combatants would fight until the last boy/girl was standing or until one of them admitted defeat. After the fight, the winner would declare victory and the loser would accept defeat. The loser wasn't vindictive; he or she accepted the humiliation and learned to deal with defeat. In some cases, the winner and loser became friends and allies afterward.

I always had a desire to work. Although I was an only child, my mother wanted to ensure that I was self-dependent, so I would clean up the house on weekends, rake the yard, mow the yard, and work at church. I guess what I'm saying is that my parents taught me a work ethic that I have not been able to duplicate for my kids. By not giving me everything I desired, they fueled a desire in me to go out and be creative to make money. My mother took me to farms to pick peas and okra during the summer. Picking the peas was backbreaking and if you had to pick okra, then you better grease yourself with Vaseline because the outer coat of okra had residue that would stick like pins. I knew right then that there was a better way of earning a living, and that way was good grades.

My first real job was as a dishwasher at Golden Corral, an honest job but not glamorous at all. Everyone had a uniform except me. I wore jeans and a red apron with a paper hat on my head. That was a life-changing event, because I could not see myself doing that for the rest of my life.

I finished high school in 1982 with a scholarship in hand, caused no problems at home or school, and was fortunate to have parents who had decent jobs. It would seem obvious that I would get a brand-new car for a graduation present. WRONG, that didn't happen. I didn't get a new car for graduation, but was told that I would be receiving my dead uncle's 1965 four-door Impala made of solid steel for being a good kid.

Life Lesson VI: *"Never allow people to place limitations on you."*

During my junior and senior years, a couple of college football scouts paid me a visit. I wasn't sure where I wanted to go to college, but Tennessee State was on the list. (My father and father-in-law attended TSU.) I was an average student, thin in stature, decent athletic ability but not a top recruit. I received a couple of 1-AA or mid-level college offers to play football, but in one of the best decisions of my life, I decided on Albany State College (ASC), my hometown college. I finished high school early and enrolled in Albany State during the spring quarter. I had come full circle, starting at an all-black elementary, going to mostly white junior and senior high schools, and finishing at an HBCU.

For the first time in eighteen years, I was in an all-black learning and social environment. This was truly a culture shock for me because growing up in a mixed educational setting and doing OK, you tend to think that you are at the top of the heap in your race. I think I was a little arrogant coming to ASC and in the back of my mind thought that this school was inferior to mixed colleges. What a rude awakening for me. I soon found out that there were some brothers and sisters walking that campus whose intellectual capacity far exceeded my own. I got to see firsthand the makings of doctors, dentists, bankers, CEOs, military giants, chemists, teachers, writers, political movers, and administrators, many of whom were told that they wouldn't amount to much in life. You see, I got an opportunity that so many of us who attended an HBCU fail to realize. I got an opportunity to learn more about my culture, I got an opportunity to socialize with people who had dreams of being difference makers in this world, and I got an opportunity to prove wrong the people who believe that you were limiting yourself by attending a HBCU. I also got an opportunity to see the most beautiful and smartest women around.

My freshman year was an interesting experience. I started at free safety or defensive back on the football team and by the beginning of the fall quarter had accumulated thirty credit hours. I was elected to the student government association, so I got a chance to mingle with some of the upperclassmen. My first and last year of playing football was not a good experience; we had some young talent, but most of the sophomores, juniors, and seniors woefully lacked the mental and physical abilities to compete at the college level. The program when I arrived was under funded (our weight room consisted of a classroom with a few concrete weights) and not what I was accustomed to, coming from a competitive high school program. We lost every game except one, and lost a player to heatstroke.

My high school teammates and I had taken pride in how we dressed. We wore dress pants, dress shoes, and dress shirts with ties to school on a frequent basis. This was not the case with the football team at ASC. Most of the players lacked the drive to go to class or care about their appearance. We had very good talent at the freshman level; it was just a matter of time before all the pieces would come together. After my freshman year, the coach turned the program around and won many conference championships.

During that season, I remained active on campus and observed the different fraternities. My father was an Alpha and I would have followed his path but the Alphas on campus didn't appeal to me nor did they seem to fit my personality. I was looking for an extended family. I was an only child, and desperately wanted to be in an organization where they called each other brother. After canvassing the four major fraternities, I chose to pledge Kappa Alpha Psi. They seemed to fit me and I them. During my pledge period, I learned a lot about myself as a person, who I would trust, who I couldn't trust, who had the interest of my well-being, who was dedicated to the cause of the fraternity, and who just wanted the benefits. I think my pledge period was no different than anyone who pledged in the early eighties and before—lots of hazing, some humiliation, and a lot of fun.

During that time, I developed a close bond with my line brothers, but especially close relationships with a couple of the older brothers. I had and continue to have a great amount of respect for a couple of those brothers who treated me fairly and became great mentors and role models. I was later elected Polemarch (president) for two consecutive terms and pledged that I would never allow some of the physical hazing that was dished to me to be dished to the future pledges. I put my heart and soul into the fraternity; I was a leader by example but did a poor job of governing my chapter.

While I was being all that I could be in Kappa Alpha Psi, I stopped playing football. When offered a three-year ROTC scholarship, I took it without hesitation. The military sent me to ROTC basic camp and that was a breeze since I'd been prepared all of my life by my parents' disciplinary ways. I excelled in ROTC, enjoyed the discipline and especially the free ride through college. No more waiting in the hot sun outside the gym or cafeteria to register. If you attended a non-HBCU, you probably won't understand that comment. For those who didn't attend an HBCU, the administrators for some reason thought that standing in line would develop patience and character. Therefore, they always rejected technology that could make registration a breeze. Now, all I had to do was show up and get my classes and the military did the rest, plus pay me $100 per month and $175 per quarter for books. The military commitment put a halt to my aspirations of owning a clothing store, so I continued in my major even though I would not apply a business degree in the military. My fraternity brothers had great aspirations: one wanted to be a dentist, another a doctor, and another a gynecologist. I just wanted to graduate, pay Uncle Sam back, and get that clothing store.

I will never forget the story of one of my mentors. Hank grew up in Albany on the rougher side of town, with many siblings in a single-parent home. He was always smart but mischievous and in trouble. A high school teacher told him that he would never amount to anything. Hank finished ASC and Tulane University to become one of the few black neurosurgeons in the nation.

As I went through school, I became more appreciative of my heritage. I truly believed that I was just as good as anyone else. I dismissed those subliminal messages from past educators and TV and radio personalities who paint this picture that black folks can't be educated to the same level as other races. I now believed that an HBCU could produce quality competitive professionals and if you don't, then think again. You don't have to look far and you can see the HBCU grads doing their thang. Look at the former Secretary of Education Rod Paige, Jackson State grad; Brown University President Dr. Ruth Simmons, Dillard University grad; tycoon Oprah Winfrey, Tennessee State University grad; former Virginia Governor Douglas Wilder, Virginia Union grad and Atlanta Mayor Shirley Franklin, Howard University grad. The list goes on and on. HBCUs were necessary back in the day and are just as necessary and relevant today; they truly know how to turn coal into diamonds.

While I was in school, I got a chance to reconnect with my roots. That includes the dollar parties where you had the cheapest beer and red Kool-Aid spiked with 100 percent golden grain alcohol; football games filled with the aroma of barbecue and fried fish and where people don't find the nearest exit for the bathroom during halftime but come out of the woodwork to pay attention to every dance move by the band and shake 'em up girls;

studying your butt off to pass that exit exam or one of your core courses. That includes being broke most of the month but when those refund checks come in, celebrating and feasting; going to Golden Corral or whatever local steak chain restaurant had that ninety-nine-cent special on Wednesdays (meat patty, baked potato and bread). Do you remember going in gangs to the restaurant and ordering the very minimum with the ability to do a couple of miracles yourself? Instead of five loaves of bread and a few fish to feed the multitude, you did it with two baskets of hot buttery bread, splitting a baked potato into fourths and cutting the steak patty in small samples so that everyone had a piece. Instead of turning water to wine for a feast, you turned two pitchers of iced water into three pitchers of the best-tasting lemonade.

I also remember one of our deans who would speak to the incoming freshmen and exclaim, "if it is to be then it is up to me" and "if it is to be then it is truly up to you." I learned early in life that nobody owes you anything; my parents showed me that by giving me what I needed; what I wanted had to be earned.

Life Lesson VII: "There was probably someone before you who made great achievements in your field. Look to them for inspiration when in doubt about your own abilities. Kick over the rocks to find them if they are not readily apparent."

As I approached my senior year in college, it was time for me to buckle down and seriously think about what I was going to do after the military. I chose a branch of the Army because it seemed kinda manly and because many of my fraternity brothers chose that same branch. I would say that my commissioning as a second lieutenant and graduation were probably the proudest moments for my parents. From their perspective, they had accomplished their parental mission and had set the stage for me to do whatever I so desired in life and they felt good, as any parent would. More importantly, they knew that they had their lives back and could do the things that they longed to do as a couple.

After graduation, I immediately reported to Fort Knox, Kentucky, for my basic course. I happened to be the only black in a class of some fifty officers... so here we go again, full circle. I have always believed that history or lack thereof can be a key factor for someone's success or stagnation. A little history; only and most powerful men in the military, those who maneuver or control combat forces, belong in two of the nineteen or so branches in the Army. The Division Commander (commands approximately 18,000 soldiers) of forces that liberate countries and those that commit those forces are usually Infantry or Armor Officers. They are known and revered as war fighters. The men who lead the divisions and higher units will be some of the best this nation has to offer, men of Colin Powell's pedigree: determined, articulate, graceful, and intelligent.

As I went through my basic course and attended class in one of the many auditoriums or mega-classroom facilities, I never saw a painting of a black armor unit or black cavalry or armor soldier. You might say, so what? This is an extremely important concept to grasp. If you're introduced to a relatively foreign environment such as the military on a full-time basis, are outnumbered in your profession by 2 to 100, must assimilate with others, and learn or relearn a culture so that you can be included in conversations, then it becomes important to know that you are not the first one to go up against the odds. It can be reassuring to see that others before you had some success in this field and were recognized for their contribution. I don't think they intentionally (or at least I hope they didn't) left out the great contributions of black units such as the Buffalo Soldiers of the 9th and 10th Cavalry or the 761st "Black Panther" Tank Battalion unit in World War II. According to *World War II* magazine's January 1998 issue:

The 761st became the first African American armored unit to enter combat during an assault on the French towns of Moyenvic and Vic-sur-Seille. Staff Sergeant Ruben Rivers won a Silver Star for his heroic action in braving direct enemy fire to remove a roadblock that could have seriously delayed the American offensive. He was severely wounded in action on November 15, 1944, but refused medical evacuation so that he might stay with his company. When their advance was stopped by enemy fire at Bougaltroff, France, on this date, Rivers' tank helped cover the company's withdrawal. He was killed and the other crewmen were injured when their tank was hit by enemy fire. Although no WWII Medals of Honor were awarded at the time to African Americans, researchers later determined that at least seven and possibly more black servicemen deserved this award. One of these men was Rivers, who was posthumously awarded the Medal of Honor in January 1997.

I think that if I had seen only one black soldier— I would have only needed one—on the walls of those auditoriums; I think I would have been inspired even more. More importantly, I think this absence could have a very negative affect on the majority or white officers. I call it "breeding a superiority complex." I don't think it was intentional, but when people constantly see figures from the past who look like them, who are revered and are displayed on walls for all to see then I'm sure it crosses their mind that their kind are the only ones who can be successful in that profession. Otherwise, there would surely be a painting with a black unit, officer or soldier on the wall. Think about it; it sends a powerful message.

Life Lesson VIII: "When you were a child you acted like a child. When you become an adult, act like one."

After completing the basic course, I was assigned to Fort Stewart, Georgia, for a three-year tour. Fort Stewart is located in the southeast portion of the state near Savannah.

Upon arrival, I was immediately assigned to an armor unit and was escorted by my commander to the motor pool to meet the battalion commander. When we arrived in the motor pool, a black officer approached me and we exchanged greetings. My commander later asked me if I knew that officer before our meeting and I told him no. He then told me to stay away from him.

My first real experience in a unit was exciting, scary, fun, life changing, and awakening. You see, for the first time in my life I earned a paycheck that would have to suffice throughout the month. There was no asking Mom or Dad for help; I had too much pride. I was an adult, a man, and that meant taking care of my responsibilities. I was responsible for my own actions and had to be a role model/leader for fifteen men and accountable for millions of dollars worth of equipment. I was ultimately responsible for their training for a potential war (this is no different than for any other officer, but certainly a different mind-set and large responsibility for a twenty something year old). Through my observations, I quickly picked up on the handful of black officers in command or key leadership positions in the combat arms units within the division;

there were only a handful, and at times, you could count the number on your thumb or index finger.

I also noticed that there were no second chances for a black officer, you were already prejudged and you either got it right or you were doomed, similar to a black quarterback in the NFL. I did my best to learn my job, hone my skills, attend social functions, and look the part of an officer. Here is where the black officer I met fits in this puzzle; he showed me everything not to do as an officer. I'll call him Mo to keep his identity unknown, but after my commander told me to stay away from him, the curiosity and the fact that we resided in the same apartment complex on post made that kinda difficult. Ole Mo found me within a couple of days and insisted that he show me the ropes since I was a brand-new officer on post. Within a two-month span, ole Mo made a pass at a soldier's wife and walked outside of his apartment to the common area with nothing covering his flabby body. When I asked him where his clothes were, he replied, "They are in the dryer and I'm going to get them out." He received a reprimand from a senior officer for hanging out at the local Kmart with his military shirt un-tucked and his military hat cocked to the side and, to top it off, burned rubber on his motorcycle going from 0 to 40 miles per hour in 1.23 seconds while traveling in a 15 mile per hour area, all in front of the commanding general.

Ole Mo did the ultimate in my book, which was to bring a young lady of the opposite race with whom he was not in a serious relationship to a formal function and, oh, by the way, he showed up late to the function. You might think that I'm prejudiced or judgmental, but I think I'm a realist and in the early '80s, we all did a double take at interracial couples, as that was taboo in the South. Some of the subtle things that I noticed that could doom one's career or cast a negative light on a black officer were the accessories that one would place on his car (the crown air fresheners, the jet black tinted windows, the rope chain license plates), attendance at a social function in a matching polyester short set with dress shoes, multiple necklaces, flashy jewelry, and an appearance at functions with a different woman for each event. These along with other stereotypical manners don't bode well in the eyes of the people who make decisions about your career.

Because I had a father who taught me how to dress conservatively but mainstream and parents who took me to events where I had to dress in business or formal attire and socialize, I faired pretty well during those events. It's amazing that some supervisors can't or won't see the potential you have or the great performance you exhibited because they are hung up over your style as an individual. I quickly learned to restrain my style of dress when invited to social events; this was not the time to try the latest fashion trend. I learned to be knowledgeable about current events and other types of music, I learned to screen very carefully any female I would invite to a social, I learned to leave my car just the way it came from the factory, and I learned to never turn down an invite. One lesson that I didn't get was to seek out successful black officers in my field who were senior to me; there was so much that I could have learned from them.

Life Lesson IX: "Stop worrying/complaining about what you don't have and take pride in what you do have."

Halfway through my tour at Fort Stewart, I was fortunate and blessed to be hounded by a financial planner named Gary. I will never forget Gary because he was placed in my life to change it in a positive way. Gary represented a financial planning company that catered to the military and, boy, did I need some help in this area. Gary was a middle-aged white man who was a retired military officer and had settled down in Hinesville to enjoy life. Gary had a passion for making money and for helping young officers help themselves by getting them financially prepared for the future.

He had many horror stories about colonels and generals who achieved great things in the military but squandered their money. I was living from check to check; credit cards maxed to the limits and not a dime in a savings account. Gary called me and called me to attend a seminar and I kept resisting and resisting because I just couldn't see how he could help me without giving me some free money to get me out of my bind. I finally attended, first, because they were serving a free meal and it was that time of month when weenies and pork and beans get old and second, because I was tired of the phone calls.

I attended the seminar and signed up for a personal meeting with Gary and that is when my life changed. You see, Ole Gary, having traveled the path I was on, could see right through my façade or even into my bank account and knew there was nothing in my account but zeroes proceeded by no other numbers. Gary took off the polite veneer and told me straight up as a father would to a disobedient son, "If you think you gonna have the nice things you want later in life the way your saving money, then you're smoking crack. And, oh, by the way, if you think that you will retire from the military, you better think again cause ain't no guarantee that you'll make it that far."

So, Ole Gary commenced to humbling me, and I was all ears on his plan to help myself. I did what he said and I thank God for bringing him into my life because he showed me that I could be financially disciplined and that I deserved everything that other folks had.

Life Lesson X: "You owe more than a thank you and homecoming visit to an institution that shaped and molded you into a better human being."

During my last year at Fort Stewart, I met the woman who took my breath away. She and I had a lot in common, and after a year and half we exchanged vows. A year later, our first child was born and she has turned into a wonderful young lady. We moved on to Fort Knox for six months so that I could attend a course and shortly thereafter, we were headed to Germany for a three-year tour.

Germany was a fascinating place, a clean and beautiful country, and we all enjoyed living there. Out of the three years that we lived in Germany, there are two lessons that I want to share. First, the German people are efficient. I think we Americans are just as efficient; however, in Germany, there is no stigma attached to a particular line of work. If you are a sanitation worker or garbage man, that line of work is viewed as just as important as a teacher, pilot, or doctor; it can be seen by the pride those workers take in wearing their uniform or the respect they give to all workers. The people take pride of their possessions and where they live; therefore, the yards are kept up, no trash in the streets and everything in its rightful place. I would say that no matter what income level family or housing area you go to, it all would be clean.

The second lesson I learned is that most people are good; it's just the few who are straight-up evil or bad who can influence a group of people. I couldn't have found a nicer and generous man who had my interests at heart than my first commander in Germany. All I have to say is that he gave me a chance plus a second chance when I didn't meet the standards; I'll never forget him.

Our tour ended with the birth of my son and we were on our way to South Carolina where I would teach ROTC at South Carolina State University. Upon our arrival in the United States, our parents picked us up from Charleston, South Carolina, and the next day we headed to my wife's hometown in Georgia.

That morning, my father told me how proud he was of me and that he loved me. Later that day, my wife and I found my father dead in her parents' bathroom. My father died at an early age, fifty-seven, but I couldn't have been more blessed than to have a man of his stature to be a consistent role model, to demonstrate by his actions how a man takes care of his family and how a man treats a woman. When it rains, it pours; a month later, I lost a dear aunt and biological grandfather, and two months after those losses my wife lost her father. I didn't know until after their deaths that both our fathers attended Tennessee State University, both were members of Alpha Phi Alpha fraternity, both had short stints in the military, both were the senior sibling in their family, and both were educators.

While at SCSU, I earned a master's in individual and family development, a relatively new but very interesting field. It was an easy study, but I did learn or reinforce my theories on people. During my studies, I had a wonderful professor (an elderly white woman) who was smart, articulate, and knowledgeable in her field. In one of my classes, we were studying/discussing the various methods of punishment for children. She started out by discussing the various methods, spanking, corporal, time out, and removal of privileges. She was a time-out advocate and began telling us how time out or taking away privileges should be the preferred method of punishment. She thought of Doctor Spock as the god for raising a family. (The late

Doctor Spock wrote many books on how to parent and probably wouldn't agree with spanking, but would agree with something that wouldn't have the potential to cause bodily harm.) I guess you know that I couldn't wait until she had a break in a sentence so that I could give her my two cents. I told her that I and many other people were spanked. I didn't get spankings; I got whippin's with my daddy's belt, with my mother's shoe, with my belt, with a tree limb, with a fraternity paddle, with an extension cord, or with whatever was around to tear my rear end up. Through all those whippin's, I and many others turned out fine. I told her that time out works for certain people, but in the African American community, we understand "if you spare the rod you will spoil the child."

I think the application of discipline for one culture cannot work for all cultures, and that is what I think has been a factor in the demise in some of our black children. You know as well as I that back in the day if you misbehaved, the nearest adult would tear you up and then report you to your parents who in turn who would tear you up again. Not anymore. I will talk about this further later in the book.

In addition to earning a master's, I got an opportunity to work with some of the best young adults around, ROTC cadets, and work with some of the best coworkers such as a good friend of mine, Charles Hicks. They made me extremely proud of serving at a HBCU. A controversial issue that seemed to divide the state while I was there was the Confederate flag atop of the capitol building. Since I was paying South Carolina taxes, I just didn't or couldn't understand how that flag was representing me or any other minority group in the state. For those that don't know, the state flag of South Carolina is a white palmetto tree on a blue background but at the capitol, the American flag was on top, followed by the state flag, followed by the Confederate flag. Now, this was 1994, and the Confederate flag was finally taken down some years later. One would think that twenty-six years after Martin Luther King's death that the symbols of divisiveness wouldn't be icons on a public building.

Because I was a nosy person, I soon learned some of Orangeburg's secrets and one was that Strom Thurmond had a daughter who attended SCSU. It was revealed after his death almost twelve years later that he had a daughter from a black woman. Additionally, I learned from one of my white counterparts at SCSU that the local white folks desperately wanted the college to pack up and go to another town, like it was some kind of circus. This was no different than the locals in my hometown who wanted my university to merge with the junior college, so I knew the deal.

Life Lesson XI: "Open your eyes; civilization exists outside the United States."

After three years in South Carolina, it was time to move on. Because I was not on track with half of my peers, my choices of assignment were not the prime for career progression. Therefore, I chose an assignment that would benefit me as well as my family. Off we went to Panama and that's not Panama City, Florida, but the country.

I spent the first six months in Panama by myself. Those six months were spent working and getting to know the culture. I met black Panamanians and white Panamanians that declared that they were neither black nor white but Panamanian. But when you really take a critical look, you can see through the façade, you easily see who has the managerial jobs and who does the menial type jobs.

Also, as an American, you realize quickly how arrogant you are, thinking that everyone wants to get in a boat and live in the United States. I talked with several Panamanians who weathered Noriega's fury, and they wouldn't want to live anywhere in the world. I got a chance to live in a developing country that was just as proud of its history and culture. The not-so-prime assignment turned into a blessing when my family arrived and got a taste of paradise. Panama was paradise with the beautiful weather, cheap food, and great facilities on post. My wife loved it even more because we had a maid who cleaned our house twice a week for only $60 per month. We bought steaks for her to eat during lunch or take home as a bonus for her hard work. Our neighbors had live in maids who were paid $160 to $200 per month; however, my wife chose the option of having one on a part-time basis.

After my family arrived, I was transferred to a new assignment within Panama. I was given oversight of a unit exchange program that would take a small delegation and me to countries in South and Central America. As a result, I would travel to Chile, Colombia, El Salvador, Argentina, Ecuador, Venezuela, and Belize. Some lessons learned while living and traveling through these countries: 1. Not everyone is trying to get to the United States. 2. Americans are the most arrogant folks on this planet and, that includes me. We arrive in a foreign land and don't even try to learn the language; we expect to eat only American type dishes such as McDonald's or KFC. We look down on the poor of the country and don't care to understand how they got there. As a matter of fact, we don't want to know why things are the way they are; all we want are the conveniences and luxuries that we had in the States. 3. The United States, with all of its problems, is the greatest nation on this earth and I wouldn't want to live anywhere else in the world.

Why do folks from other countries hate us? Let me tell you what the average Joe Blow would tell you, no studies or scientific analysis, just observing and talking with the indigenous folks. Throughout my travel, talking with and observing people it's not that they hate every American. I would say that 95 percent of Americans who visit or live abroad are a good reflection of the values and principles for which this great country stands. It's the 5 percent or less who taint the image of the U.S., it's the one of a hundred businesses in Venezuela or in some other country that pollutes the environment, or treats its employees like slaves or fails to give back to the community. It's the one of 10,000 soldiers or tourists who commits a horrendous crime against the locals. More importantly, it's the forcing of our culture on a society that wants to remain the same. This can be done by constant advertising in a country or demands from visitors such as, "How come you don't have … " "Why don't you have … " "I'm not going to stay if I don't get … ." The things we ask for are usually not necessities but our creature comforts.

After a year in paradise, it was time to move on and with great reluctance and apprehension, we were assigned and moved to Mississippi.

Life Lesson XII: "You owe it to others to give back once you've made it."

Mississippi was totally different than we expected. Even though I grew up in the Deep South, Mississippi was considered to be far behind the other Southern states. However, I quickly learned that Mississippians had done a lot of self-examination and were determined to right the wrongs of the past; I can't say the same for some of the other Southern states.

The unit to which I was assigned consisted of junior and senior officers and noncommissioned officers who went out and evaluated/trained/assisted the local National Guard units in the area (Mississippi, Alabama, and Louisiana). My commander pulled me aside during my first week to discuss working relationships or how I would/should deal with Southern white reserve officers who may not respect or have apprehensions about working with a black officer and senior trainer for the unit. Many of the reserve combat arms units in the South rarely have a black officer in their units; to have an outsider, especially a black officer, advise and evaluate them can be a bit much for some of them to swallow. He called me into his office and began to ask me about my background; what school I attended, where I was born, where I served. Typical questions; however, I could sense that there were specific, somewhat sensitive questions that he wanted to ask. As he stared me down with doubt written on his face, knowing what he wanted to discuss, I quickly stated that I was from the South and knew that it was going to be a challenge to gain the respect and credibility of the Guardsmen in that area. After I made that remark, a sigh of relief overcame him and we were off to more pertinent business.

My chance to make an impression came only a week later when all of the officers from the Mississippi and Alabama units came to our location for an exercise rehearsal. That turned out to be a very important meeting because I forged a working relationship with many of the senior officers in those units and developed a friendly relationship with many of the Alabama officers. You see, I had taken my past experiences and stereotypes and applied them across the board, not willing to really give people the benefit of doubt. What I saw in Mississippi were people who were trying their best to change the image of their state. I noticed the most respectful and courteous people in the South; everyone, black and white, would speak to you and everyone, black and white, no matter what age, always started off with "sir" or "ma'am" and responded with "yes sir" or "yes ma'am." You might not think much of that but "yes sir" or "yes ma'am" along with other good attributes can take you a long way in life.

My tour in Mississippi was relatively uneventful other than the fact I got an opportunity to see a different Southern culture. A couple of things that I will never forget about Mississippi: catfish is king and on Fridays, you better get to the local seafood restaurant early. Blues are king and I'm not talking about rhythm and blues; B.B. King is what young and old listen to. The blues festivals that are held on Mother's Day and Father's Day weekends are the talk at the barber shop for young and old; they are just as important as Christmas. People don't pronounce Miss–is–sip–pi, they pronounce it Miss–sip–i. While in Miss–sip–i, I began to really believe and live by the saying "Give back to the community." Thanking God for the many undeserved blessings, I sought out and found a program where I could mentor elementary students. You know, you always hear the religious leaders profess "it's easier/better to give than to receive." I think I take that to heart because I would much rather be in a position of giving than receiving… it's more than a mind-set.

Near the end of my tour in Mississippi, I was given a couple of choices for my next assignment.

Life Lesson XII: "An old dog CAN learn new tricks."

I requested to be transferred in the South but on the East Coast, specifically Atlanta. I thought it best to get an assignment there in preparation for retirement down the road. I was granted my wish and my family and I were off to Atlanta. It was a blessing to be only a couple of hours away from our parents. We were in the capital of the South and a haven for successful blacks, where million-dollar homes and neighborhoods that you would think would be mixed or all white were occupied by black men and women. A historical area for blacks, abundant industry, and good-paying jobs brought blacks from all over the nation looking for an opportunity. Now, don't get me wrong; Atlanta has its problems with its political leadership, crime, and traffic but, all in all, it's a very good place to live.

My first year in Atlanta was enjoyable as I continued to mentor through a program at work. I kept abreast of the local politics, followed the slaying of a sheriff in Atlanta that was perpetrated by the outgoing sheriff. I followed the scandals from the mayor's office and witnessed some of the most inept leaders in surrounding counties. Although I had a tough job in the Forces Command Operations Center, I maintained a balance, and my first year went by faster than you could snap a finger.

I and many other folks will never forget what we were doing on September 11, 2001, a life-changing event. I will never forget looking at the huge TV screens in the operations center when those planes crashed into the towers and then receiving a phone call that the Pentagon had just been struck. Our pace in the operations center went from a cruise of 50 miles per hour to a fleeting pace of sonic boom proportions. We immediately received orders from our headquarters and began preparation to deploy units somewhere. Within a week or two, we had soldiers on the ground in the Middle East and were preparing forces to invade Afghanistan. That was a proud period for me because the President emerged from this travesty to be a strong leader with a commitment to bring justice to the folks who perpetrated this cowardly act. I was all for military action to find, capture, or kill the folks behind this event.

One of the questions that the American public just couldn't understand and I think to this day leaders in the administration and elsewhere still can't reconcile is "Why did they do this?" We hadn't done anything to those folks. Many answers were given; some said they just hated us because we are free, and others said that they were crazed people who were jealous.

I don't think anybody except one or two folks understand the real reason why this attack occurred. I surely missed it until I started doing some reflection on my past travels and listening to the pundits debate the reason why. I believe those folks attacked us not because they were jealous of the United States, our freedom, constitution, our economy, or our standard of living. They attacked us because they were tired/threatened of the American culture being forced on them, they were tired of the direct American influence on their folks through our stationing of uniformed men and women in the Middle East and, yes, tired of the arrogance that we as a people display when dealing with others. You see, I can recall being stationed overseas and traveling to different countries and how I acted toward many of the indigenous people. I always wanted them to speak English, not their native tongue; I wanted the conveniences of America; I wanted to see basketball or football on the local channels, not soccer; I wanted the same nightlife that I sometimes enjoyed in America; I wanted a convenience store on every corner. Many of the things that we tolerate in America—prostitution, pornography, homosexuality, independent women, overvaluing of material possessions, or degrading music—are just outright taboo in other countries. So just imagine thousands of me, and I ain't the worse of them, in a country that is trying to preserve its traditions and its culture. Believe me, the older folks put up good resistance to the onslaught of our culture, but the young are like sheep and are easily influenced to go in a different direction. So, in addition to why I think this attack occurred, check out Amy Chua's *World on Fire;* it is so revealing as to why this happened.

The year came and went, and we were off to a good start bringing the cowards to justice. I continued my life as everyone else did.

During 2002, my church went through a meta–morphosis. We abandoned some of the traditional ways in which we worshiped and embraced new methods of worshiping. You might think so what, many churches go through this process. But this was new and life changing for me. Everywhere I have been stationed, including Germany and Panama, I always sought and found a church exactly like mine: same name, same worship methods, and same principle beliefs. For the sake of our marriage, my wife left her church to become a member of mine; I thank her every day for that sacrifice. The change in my church really opened my eyes to the traditions and customs people get so caught up in when they are indoctrinated at an early age or when they are most vulnerable. There are some ministers who rightly divide the word and there are many others who don't, but there are millions of us who don't study to show thyself approved unto God and as a result, we become totally dependent on their preaching whether right or wrong.

Through my volunteer work and activities in church, I decided that I wanted to give public office a shot after my military career and I located a leadership program that my county offered. I recommended myself, paid my tuition, and completed an outstanding program the following year. Afterward, there was no doubt that I was running; at what position and when were the only questions.

Life Lesson XIII: "Serving others is often tiring and thankless, but the inner reward of knowing that you have purpose on this earth exceeds all of the thank yous and accolades bestowed upon you."

My last year of my tour was an eventful year as well and is probably the reason why I'm writing this book. Till this point, the military had a successful campaign in Afghanistan. It looked as if we not only were going to bring the folks who perpetrated this act to justice but also would share some of the many blessings that we as a nation have received to a group of people who were deprived of their basic human rights. I always thought it prudent to restore Afghanistan into a somewhat democratic country that could be the shining jewel of democracy for the Middle East. Then the United States could boldly say, "Look at what we did to help folks in a place where we really have no strategic interests." Things were looking up until we decided to invade Iraq and for the love of me I couldn't and don't till this day understand why we went to war with Iraq. I know why we went to war: it was because of an ideological movement within the administration that led others who may have straddled the fence to believe that our mission in this world is to spread democracy, creating governments who think and act like we do.

After the successful invasion in Iraq, I was transferred to the Pentagon to work in my functional area. My family and I made a decision that I would stay in D.C. while they remained in Atlanta. This assignment would be my last assignment before retirement. The Pentagon is an awesome place to work and learn the Beltway culture; it is the largest office building in the world, employing over 22,000 people. Through my years in the military, I never knew or understood the political impact on the military until I was assigned there.

Being away from my family was one of the toughest decisions that I've had to make, but it was necessary since my kids were around friends and in a school that they enjoyed. More importantly, my wife received a career advancement that she could not pass up. To cope with the situation, I immediately immersed myself in my fraternity, specifically the Guide Right Program (Kappa League).

Kappa League is a mentorship program focusing on at-risk young men ages ten to seventeen. During the first meeting I attended, I knew this was the program that I wanted to be a part of, because it gave me an opportunity to give back. As a result, I volunteered to be the co-chair of and immediately added my touch to the program, heading it in a direction that would more greatly benefit and enrich the young men as well as their parents.

Our Kappa League outline consisted of at least one meeting per month that focused on character building, male responsibilities, and the tools needed to be successful. We would meet another weekend during the month to conduct our community service events such as feeding the homeless, cleaning up the community, or taking the young men to a sports or cultural outing. I think our monthly meetings were the best, because we got an opportunity to showcase the many talents and professions of our members. I soon realized how important it is for young men, especially young men who are being raised by a single parent, to have a male role model. These young men got an opportunity to see other successful black men, young and old, doing the things that they wanted to do. We brought in professional football and basketball players to tell them their version of success, as well as businessmen, project managers, scientists, doctors, lawyers, and military giants. More importantly, when they had men-type questions such as, "What happens to your body during puberty?" or "How should I go about meeting a young lady?" They received advice not from their thirteen-year-old friends, but from responsible men who had experienced what they were going through.

I also became involved in the community and applied for a board position on the Alexandria City Environmental committee, but was not accepted. A few months later, I applied for a citizen at-large position on the Youth Policy Committee and was accepted. While serving on the Youth Policy Committee, I was reminded of the life lesson of how important it is for people to get involved in the community in which they live. Citizen involvement really does make a difference between a good and not-so-good community. The committee I served on was chaired by the mayor and is probably one of the most influential boards since it controls funds for grants to boost youth programs in the city. The fascinating thing about Alexandria is the sense of community; everyday citizens and professionals serve on approximately thirty boards ranging from the Youth Policy Committee to Washington Birthday Parade Committee to the Aging and Elderly Board to the Beautification Board to the Housing Board. These boards and committees are designed to get citizen participation in the democratic processes within the community and, believe me, the citizens are very involved in the business of their city.

During my stay in the D.C. area, I occasionally attended Shiloh Baptist Church where my aunt and uncle Williams were members. I must say that if one wanted to model a productive church, look to the service, outreach programs and vision from Shiloh. The church had programs available for all, tennis team, HBCU Council, Nursing Club, AIDS Task Force, economic empowerment committees, mentorship programs, and the best musical organizations ever witnessed. The church exposed the membership to life's possibilities by having great men and women including Dr. Floyd H. Flake (president of Wilberforce), Juan Williams (columnist for the *Washington Post*), Dr. Bill Gray (the former congressman and former president-CEO of the United Negro College Fund), retired Rear Admiral Barry C. Black (first African American chaplain for the U.S. Senate), Marietta Simpson (Opera Singer) and a representative of the Black Secret Service organization preach, sing or say a few words. Even though there are some heavy hitters from the educational, government and private business realm who are members at Shiloh, the church remains humble as a whole and welcomes anyone no matter what stage they are in their walk of life.

I must say that living in the D.C. area exposed me to the political processes that impact people's lives more than what I could have ever imagined. It also reinforced my belief that no matter where you come from or where you went to school, if you use your God-given talents and are determined, you will succeed in America.

Now that I've shared a little of myself and probably given you some info on why I think the way that I do, let's cut through the chase and get to talking about some specific topics that I am passionate about.

Chapter II:

Going to Church or Doing Church

"The church must be reminded that it is not the master or the servant of the state, but rather the conscience of the state. It must be the guide and the critic of the state, and never its tool. If the church does not recapture its prophetic zeal, it will become an irrelevant social club without moral or spiritual authority."
Martin Luther King Jr., Strength to Love, 1963.

~What Happened to the Black Church~

THE SOUTH has long been declared the Bible Belt. You can find a church on almost every corner and now almost in every plaza in the South. Whether in the Bible Belt or on the West Coast or in Midwest, blacks found solace in the church and not too long ago, the church was the only institution where blacks could worship, govern, and discipline themselves. The church was also the community center, polling station, Red Cross, Goodwill, and homeless shelter. It was all those things that we now look for from our government.

So what happened? Did the black church fail us? I don't know if the black church failed us but I do know that the black church went through a metamorphosis after the civil rights movement that changed its direction and focus. Think about it; the black church was everything till to the end of the civil rights movement. The most respected and most powerful black men in the community were not necessarily the most educated; the ministers or elders/deacons usually wielded the most power. They were the gatekeepers to your spiritual needs and your earthly existence. If you recall, Dr. Martin Luther King, Ralph Abernathy, Malcolm X, and many other folks used their religious beliefs and more importantly their platforms to deal with the social injustices against blacks and other minorities.

Some of these men were educated and others were self-taught; the majority of the church leadership during that time consisted of the common man, the carpenter, welder, farmer, factory worker, brick mason, butcher etc. Nothing against any of these great common men, but the majority weren't visionaries but maintainers of the status quo. In other words, we lost our edge or fell behind a couple of steps due to the complacency of our church leadership in an ever-changing country. The civil rights movement utilized the church to rally people and once we had accomplished the great feat of integration, the church was no longer relevant. You see, we now had the right to go to the schools and restaurants of our choice, had gained access to many of the social organizations, and had governmental programs such as Head Start and summer youth programs that took the place of the church's mission in the past. The only thing we now needed from church was the spiritual feeding, so we thought.

In a few cases, we had churches located in the neighborhoods that were ministering to the people's need but for the most part, this type of ministering was nonexistent. As our opportunities expanded, so did the options of young talented men who may have once thought of becoming ministers and leading their own flock. They now looked to the more profitable professions, leaving a large hole to be filled by men who were intellectually challenged to transition the church into the new society. In many cases, our churches were left behind with an aging membership devoid of any ideas to connect with the younger generation. This void caused us to be blind to the potentials of church community service programs, land ownership, economic viability in the community, education of our own and political power.

Further exacerbating this problem was the migration of blacks to the suburbs. As a result of the gains from the civil rights movement, many blacks who could afford to leave the inner city did so, leaving the older and poorer blacks behind. I would speculate that many of the blacks who moved to the suburbs commuted to and from worship services within the inner city until a church was established for them in the suburbs. The folks who moved to the suburbs left behind many of the social problems that affected blacks, only to see them on TV or hear about them during worship services.

More importantly, many of the blacks who had the resources to make an impact on the social ills were now distant to those issues; they don't hit home if you live, work, and learn in a safe and comfortable environment. We focused on up scaling the church across the street or outbuilding each other to see who had the most opulent edifice instead of finding commonalities to address the social problems in the community. In some cases, we were afraid to step out on faith and as a result, we maintained the same building, same services, and same thought processes while others were seeking creative ways to bring others to the church. I think we as a people forgot about how important the church could be to our very existence.

~The Divided House~

Blacks are the most churchgoing folks in this country, according to a Gallup Poll. Four out of every ten blacks attend church on a regular basis compared with three out of every ten whites. In the South, there is a church on almost every corner. The folks who attend these churches rarely know the other folks in nearby churches; nor do they come together to worship or to deal with a crisis in the community they serve. You know what I'm talking about, this group who won't worship or work with this group and vice versa. I know this because there was a black

Catholic church thirty yards next to my home church, but we didn't worship together nor did we pool our resources to tackle the many problems in our neighborhood. I've attended other churches that are within walking distance of two or three different churches and they too have never interacted.

I can even recall an incident where the kids from my church were no longer allowed to play in a church basketball league because they had won so many games. A church youth director stopped a game and canceled the remainder of our games because our team was winning. His rationale was that the other teams needed a chance to win as well. That certainly wasn't the real reason. It was all about competition and wanting to be recognized. You probably know many instances where one church won't participate in a community event unless it was allowed to run the event. All you have to do is listen to the church announcements, and I can almost guarantee you that if you're in one faith, then the only news that will be mentioned is news about the churches within that faith. In many cases, there are three or four different churches in that community but you will rarely see them working together or sharing information about the major events in their church. There can be a crisis within that community, and many of the churches will approach the problem by themselves or totally ignore it.

The reasoning behind this approach is that many of our church leaders have allowed the human factors of competition and recognition to become dominant and have minimized cooperation, selflessness, and humbleness. This is evidenced by many of our churches trying to build the most opulent edifice or creating titles for their leaders or ensuring they have the best-dressed pastor with the most expensive car. The churches located near each other that fail to interact at some level are engaging in a competition that is not healthy for the community or its members. If that is not the reason, then it could be because different faiths may not agree on the methods of service/worship. However, that barrier should be broken when there is good that could result for all. It's interesting to note that when the Klan was attacking the marchers (I'm sure they were of different faiths) in Selma, the marchers didn't have a problem assembling in a nearby church for safety. And when it was time to rally forces to protest, they certainly didn't look at whose church the meeting was going to take place. I'm not the expert on whose religion is right, but I will tell you this: all that I've learned tells me that the most important thing is to love thy God with all thy might and, secondly, love thy neighbor as thyself.

If those commandments were so important that a prophet wrote them on behalf of God, then why don't we utilize the resources that God has given to us to help our fellow man? That is one way of prophesying our love to God. I grew up in a church with God-fearing people who wanted nothing but the best for me. I can truly say that this was a congregation of loving human beings who interpreted and followed the Scriptures strictly. I believed the principle of oneness/singularity of churches until I got older and started thinking and wondering about the person who goes to another church but is the most generous and loving person you could ever meet or the person who devotes all of his or her time doing the things Christ did while on earth. No longer is the title of the church so important as the character of the person and what the church does for the glory of God, including the application of the two most important commandments.

Just because you say you are saved and believe you are in the right church doesn't mean you are bound for heaven if you're not doing the things that will glorify God. Because of this, I now refuse to pass judgment on other people's faith, look down on their beliefs, or disassociate myself from them strictly based on their religious beliefs. I'll leave the judging to God. Not only did we divide ourselves based on the shade of our skin, but we have further divided ourselves in the name of religion.

~Burying Your Talents~

The church I grew up in was located, as many others are, in the heart of the middle- to lower-income black neighborhoods with no community programs/facilities nearby. I can certainly say that anyone who attended my church was well received. If you attended on a regular basis or if you became a member, then you could benefit from some of the programs/services that were afforded to members. This is not an anomaly; this happens in many of our congregations to this day. Removed from my church some twenty years, I can now look back and see we did not maximize the talents and resources within our congregation. There were so many more programs and services that we could have provided to the community that would have subsidized or supplanted the meager government entitlements and dealt with the many social ills that affect the black community.

I think this is a result of short-term rather than strategic/long-term vision from men who meant well but just weren't business savvy. I use my church as an example but I think my church happens to be the typical/traditional black church as it relates to services and programs during that time. The black church missed a golden opportunity to provide daycare programs that were either free of charge or charged minimal fee, community facilities that provided a safe place for children to learn and play, job training services taught/sponsored by church members, shuttle services for the elderly, money management and home buying seminars, tutoring assistance, and medical and dental screening.

Some black ministers will say that the church is not a fraternal organization or community club; however, I think they have it all wrong. The church should be an organization whose people are close-knit, and the church should be the entity looking out for the interests of the people within its community. I once heard a lady on a talk show remark that the black church has failed us; she gave examples of the so-called churches whose doors were never open unless there was a worship service and concluded that because of this, people were failing to minister to the people's needs. She went on to state that if a person wanted to have a graduation celebration or some type of family event, then usually the local church was not an option, first, because the church leadership probably wouldn't allow it unless you were a member; second, because the cost to use the church was just as expensive as a rental hall; and lastly, the church leadership worshipped the facility and wouldn't allow any event unless it was a worship service, wedding or funeral. My thought is, why not use the church facilities (within reason) as a gathering place? If enlightened citizens wanted to have an event to celebrate something positive, why shouldn't the local church be the first place they turn? Why should we have to look solely at the government to deal with the daycare crisis, homeless situation, high unemployment rate, job training etc. when we have the resources and talents within our churches.

Now, here are a few things that eat me alive. The percentage of black teachers in the public school system is around 6 percent of all teachers, according to the National Education Association. I would like to think that at least 3 percent or approximately 120,000 of those teachers attend worship service on a regular basis. If that be the case, then why are some of our kids so far behind? Why don't all or most of these folks minister by forming a tutorial service free of charge at their local church? I would also venture to say that we have a good percentage of LPNs and RNs who attend church on a regular basis and maybe one or two doctors attend the church as well. Then why don't we have free medical screenings for the community on a regular basis? This would be a form of ministry. I know we have some successful young men and women who attend church on a regular basis, because they sure drive up in the latest expensive car and dress with the finest clothes. If this is the case, then why do we have so many of our young men and women without role models? A mentorship program that meets on a frequent basis could be another ministry. We have elderly members who are looking to give back and wouldn't mind devoting some of their time providing daycare services or tutoring or assisting the homeless. Why not establish a ministry to utilize the talents of these wise and seasoned saints?

In my home near Atlanta there is a church that actually has these types of programs. I haven't stepped a foot in the door, but I've heard about the wonderful workout facilities and gym that are open for the public, all the church asks you to do is to register (not become a member) and abide by its rules. The doctors and nurses devote a portion of their time to give free screenings to the members and the community. I know this because it is advertised in the local paper. It is possible to do all these things; it's just a matter of folks doing church more than going to church.

~The Moral Conscience of the Community~

The black church has to be the moral conscience of the community; Dr. King stated that it had to be *the guide and the critic of the state.* If you grew up in the church, especially in the South, then you can recall the fire and brimstone sermons that were preached at least once a month. The preacher would always have a catchy theme and would start by stating that he would "have to step on some toes" to deliver his message. He would then begin by quoting or reading Scripture about the wrongdoings of a character in the Bible and how that person was condemned to eternal damnation. From that point, he dissected how that same social ill or individual sin would cause harm to the believer and community as a whole. All eyes and ears were focused on the minister as he scared people straight with his fiery and animated delivery.

The fire and brimstone messages were based on the social issues of that community or, on occasion, national issues. These messages were praised by the older folks in the church who loved the sermons because the messages usually didn't apply to them or reinforced their moral standards. You would hear many amens from the brothers in the amen corner and the sisters occupying their chosen spots on the third and fourth pews. The only time that the preacher stepped on everyone's toes was when he preached about giving and that was only twice a year; after New Year's and right before summer vacation. If the message was about the sin you committed the other night or day, then you would say to yourself, "He must have seen me! How could he talk about me like that in public?" If the theme wasn't about you, then you sighed relief and looked around the church to see who was getting edgy or looked nervous, because they had to be the one who he was preaching about.

These fire and brimstone sermons covered every possible perceived social ill. I even remember a sermon I thought was directed at me because I just had a fraternity tattoo inscribed on my arm. The theme of the sermon was about joining secular organizations and defiling the temple of God, your body. I must say that the ministers in those days didn't care about coddling their members; they didn't care if you were offended; and they certainly didn't care if their messages drove folks away. In their mind's eye, they were the conscience of the community through God and they believed that was their purpose on earth. Although we received more than our fair share of the fire and brimstone messages back in the day, I know there was some benefit to the community as a whole because moral parameters were established. You knew that your local minister wasn't going to sway from the moral analogies and interpretations of the teachings of the Bible, and that the new social trends that were perceived to be harmful to the community (blacks) would be challenged by Scripture and verse. These sermons were inculcated in the minds of the believers, and they in turn would rebuke or challenge anyone outside of the church who felt compelled to mandate a social trend as acceptable.

Look at the Catholic Church today, which is in a dilemma on how to handle gay priests. How did this faith sway from its teachings, or did it even speak up when confronted with this social trend? I will say, just as the Catholic Church is faced with this dilemma today, so did the black church go through a period of absent moral consciousness.

Instead of facing the social trends and ills such as single parenthood, black on black crime, degrading rap music, discipline of our children, or lack of taking personal responsibility, we as a church kept quiet, all in the name of maintaining membership and keeping people happy. Many of our ministers and leaders deflected the problems facing our folks on the government while failing to admonish personal shortcomings. The government seemed to be the choice target since it didn't occupy a pew nor did it give tithes; it became the transparent devil in which all folks (ministers and congregation) could hurl their frustrations without having to look inward. As a result, we had evil running our communities while the law-abiding citizen or believer was trapped in his or her house, afraid to venture out. Or we were constantly subjected to the affects of a race crippled with the epidemic of crack and degrading rap music or saddened by the males of our community who happily shirked their parental responsibilities while leaving many of our women with the burdens of providing for and raising a family. Until we have ministers who are willing to step on toes, confront the perceived detrimental social trends, and at the same time be compassionate to their people's needs then we will continue to have an absence of moral consciousness.

~The Church is a Hospital, not a Welfare Office~

A good hospital is constantly busy with patients who have minor injuries to life-threatening illnesses. The good hospitals are manned with great doctors and nurses who have studied and know their craft. The good hospitals don't discriminate against a person's race, religion, culture, or social status; the only thing that the good hospitals are concerned about is making the person who walked through the door well. The really good hospitals don't even care if you have insurance; they will admit you and deal with the payment later. The good hospitals are always open, and their staffs are looking for innovative ways of treating a disease or injury that has caused great pain or death in the community. Once you've been admitted and treated at the good hospitals, the doctors and nurses will ensure that you know how to deal with any future or recurring problems before you are released. They want to ensure that you are able to help yourself first before you have to see them again. If you are ill and you can't help yourself, then they certainly want you to know that their offices remain wide open for you.

The traits of a good hospital are the essentials of a good church. People within the community need to know that they can call on the leadership when their soul is sick and need a diagnosis and treatment.

The people in the community need to know that they will not be judged on their social status or their lifestyle, and they need to know that they do not have to pay to receive ministering. More importantly, the people in the community and in the church need to know that because you dress well, drive a nice car, own a beautiful house, and have a good job does not necessarily mean that you are spiritually well.

Sometimes we can become judgmental to the point that we turn away folks who might not live within our so-called standards or who might not be as educated as us; remember, they have the same right that we do to receive spiritual feeding. This could be one of the ways the black church has failed us. Do you recall or remember a so-called saint at your church who didn't drink, smoke, or do anything that was considered an overt sin, but was the most judgmental person in the church? You might know more than one. I'm talking about the person who would say something like this to the other members about a visitor: "You know she is the biggest ho around, she got the nerve to come in God's house" or "You know he is an alcoholic, he's probably drunk right now" or "The way they dressed, looked like they just came from the club" or "They ain't got nothing better to put on."

I know we have members like this, because I've heard and seen them. At times I've passed judgment on a person at the same time I was dying spiritually from the sin that I had committed; however, my illness was disguised by the job I had, the clothes I wore, and the education I had attained.

The good churches educate and remind their membership that the church is the spiritual community hospital and although the members feel that they have a good bill of spiritual health, they need constant checkups and treatment on a regular basis. As a result, the membership welcomes with open arms the drug addict, the prostitute, the alcoholic, the thief, the uneducated, the jobless, the homeless, or whoever out there needs healing. As a matter of fact, they go out of their way to find these folks, not to preach about eternal damnation but to tell them about the hospital and ultimate doctor who can heal all of their illnesses.

The good churches have members who are actively involved, no matter what secular skills they possess. If you are breathing, then the good churches will find a way to stimulate you to work because they know that it takes a collective effort to stay viable. The good churches have ministers who tell their members that yes, the church is the hospital but not the welfare office. These ministers inform folks that God has blessed them with talent, whether it is a single talent or multiple talents; he has equipped them to do something positive for themselves and make a difference in the world. They also utilize the examples and instruction within the Bible to deal with certain situations; I call it self-help and not conservatism. These ministers are believers that God can do all things while at the same time believe that God has passed certain abilities to us to deal with our problems and when we've exhausted our means, then we should turn to him like a child to a parent.

This leads me to the welfare members who come only to lay their problems at the foot of the altar. Being a little judgmental myself, these are the folks who can never be found to work or never volunteer for a committee; the only time you see or hear from them is when they have a problem. Rather than seeking the help of the leadership in private, they feel quite comfortable announcing their problems in front of the congregation. I'm not talking about the members who have exhausted everything in their power to resolve an issue and then come to the congregation for prayer and help. I'm talking about the ones who haven't done anything themselves to see if they can rectify the problem. The welfare members come testifying that they can't get along with their co-workers or boss, they come because they don't have enough money to make ends meet, they come because their child is disobedient, they come because they have a health ailment, for whatever reason, big or small, they come calling on the Lord to take their cares away.

As I have sat in various congregations, I have observed that possibly some of these problems are self-induced and God has already provided the necessary tools to deal with these issues. When I hear people saying, "Oh Lawd" if you could just get me that pay raise, everything will be all right or "Oh Lawd" my boy has been acting up in school and I just don't know what to do or "Oh Lawd" they just don't treat me right at my job or school or "Oh Lawd" this life on earth is hell, people just don't treat me right.

One of these problems could be addressed by disciplining your child when young. God gave you that authority. Check out Judges 6:1-10. Another problem can be addressed by living within your means. God never intended for everyone to be rich, a lot of folks will be poor, some will be not so poor and a few will be rich. Check out Timothy 6: 6-10 or Ecclesiastes 5:10. For those who aren't treated right, then take solace in Romans 12: 17-19: *Do not repay anyone evil for evil. Be careful to do what is right in the eyes of everybody. If it is possible, as far as it depends on you, live at peace with everyone. Do not take revenge, my friends, but leave room for God's wrath, for it is written: 'It is mine to avenge; I will repay, says the Lord.* Every problem has already been addressed in the Bible.

I truly understand that God wants us to depend on him, but also think that he wants us to use the powers that he has given us first to resolve our issues. Finally, I heard a minister state that he wasn't going to waste his time or God's time asking for a new car because God gave him the intellect to figure out that he needed a steady job, down payment, and decent credit to get the luxury car he wanted. I know that's simplistic but it's also true.

~The Mega Churches~

The religious movement of the late '90s was the prosperity kick. The mega churches became so because people were looking for services/programs to deal with the social ills of our day and because some ministers fueled the belief that all people in their congregation were destined to be prosperous (materialistically) because God has so ordained. During this time, you could tune your TV to almost any religious program and hear the prosperity doctrine. I have never been a believer in this doctrine because if you live in America, then God has already made you prosperous. If you're an able-bodied man or woman living in this country, then God has already given you all the tools to make life comfortable and wonderful.

Some ministers have made themselves rich on this doctrine, and I can't see how they have benefited the community with this talk. Why am I so hard on this belief? It is because it is a smoke screen that blinds you to the things that really matter in life, such as doing your best and accepting your position in life, helping others that are less fortunate than you by giving your time and resources, and being the best citizen or parent you can be. Prosperity to me is having a loving family, a job, a place to live, access to medical and dental care, reliable transportation to get from point A to B, and peace of mind. Secondly, I'm hard on some of the mega churches because the wealth that the ministers and leaders accumulate doesn't seem commensurate to the level of community outreach from the church. I'm not against a minister owning a personal jet and several multimillion-dollar homes, but it appears to the outsider that some of that money could augment many of the programs established within the church. When you have members within the mega churches who know more about their minister's homes, cars and vacation spots than they know about the missions and outreach programs then something is wrong.

I was fortunate to hear Dr. Floyd H. Flake, president of Wilberforce University and pastor of one of the largest churches in New York, tell his story of self-help and the power of the church. He admonished and challenged the church to step outside of its traditional boundaries and do something about social ills from gentrification to educating, to become the moral backbone of the community, and to speak out on issues including degrading music and reliance on self rather than the government. His church did the impossible by buying up local property and refurbishing it to sell back to the community. I know that the mega churches make an impact, but to what degree do they make that impact?

~Getting Back to the Basics~

I've talked about the churches of the now, the mega churches, and even talked about the opportunities that my home church and other traditional churches missed. Now, I want to tell you about one thing my home church and similar traditional churches have mastered that many of the other churches I've attended haven't… and that's men taking charge of church business and providing up and front role models for young black men and women.

Years ago, it was unheard of a woman taking a leadership role in the church. But as our culture changed, so did our accommodations for women leaders in the church. Some of these changes were of necessity with the shrinking number of males attending church and some were due to a new interpretation of the Bible or an acknowledgment of the leadership roles of women in the Bible.

The traditional church, regardless of denomination, may have missed the opportunities that the self-service mega churches took advantage of or may not be all inclusive when it comes to worship but bring a sense of order that is needed so desperately in our churches and communities. Almost pushed to the brink of extinction, these churches have a commonality that needs to be emulated in most of the churches of the now. This commonality is that men are in charge of worship service, hold the leadership positions, and head up the committees. These men do so not because they are egotistical or are told to do so; they do it because the Bible teaches them that they are to be the head of the house as well as the church.

So where does this place the woman in church? It places the woman in a supporting role most of the time and in a leading role when necessary. I say that when you have men who are sound in the Scripture, then they should run church affairs (deacons/ministers/ushers/elders). But I can certainly see a woman being given leadership responsibility in whatever capacity her talents take her and the church accepts. The problem we have in most of the smaller and now churches is that 65-80 percent of the membership is female, and the remaining percentage of men are either not grounded in their faith to lead the church, worn out from serving in various capacities, or too afraid to make a religious commitment and be counted on a regular basis. Our churches and society are in desperate need of black role models, and what better way for a young lady or young man to witness the order of life than to see men taking charge of the spiritual needs of the membership? What better way to counter the negative images of the black man than to see him serving a higher authority, God? Women leaders in the church is an issue I struggle with, what's appropriate and what the Bible states. I do know that we need men of strong character and faith to be in charge.

Lastly, what's up with this relaxed standard of dress on Sunday? I know some churches chose to go to a relaxed dress standard, and even the church I currently attend has gone to this standard, but I think it has gone too far. Some people think that a person should not be judged on what he or she wears to church because God doesn't care about your outer appearance but your inner appearance. I agree to a certain extent. Sunday services should not be a fashion show; however, it's also not a place where we wear our ball game, casual Friday, and picnic clothing.

I think God expects us to present our best, and if our

best is a pair of jeans then so be it. But if our best, not what's comfortable, is a suit, dress, or pantsuit, then we should be in our best during times of worship. Back in the day, if you had a suit or dress, you wore it to church, and if it was the only one you had, then you ensured it was clean for the next service. We have made service too casual, trying to attract others; there has to be a balance, but it should not go at the expense of respecting him during our primary worship service on Sunday.

Chapter III

We Just Don't Get It When It Comes to Sports

"Unlike any other business in the United States, sports must preserve an illusion of perfect innocence. The mounting of this illusion defines the purpose and accounts for the immense wealth of American sports. It is the ceremony of innocence that the fans pay to see—not the game or the match or the bout, but the ritual portrayal of a world in which time stops and all hope remains plausible, in which everybody present can recover the blameless expectations of a child, where the forces of light always triumph over the powers of darkness." Lewis Lapham, 1935

~I Can't Put My Finger on It, But Something Is Missing~

COULD YOU imagine basketball without Michael Jordan, Dr. J, or Shaq? Think about not being able to watch players such as Walter Payton or Michael Vick on your TV sets on Sunday afternoons. What would baseball be like if we didn't have sluggers such as Hank Aaron or Barry Bonds? Can you even imagine what tennis would have been like without standouts such as Arthur Ashe or the William sisters?

For several decades, blacks and other minorities were relegated to their own leagues and were not allowed to compete for individual or national championships. Josh Gibson, John Henry Lloyd, "Smoky" Joe Williams, James Thomas "Cool Papa" Bell, and Oscar Charleston were great baseball players back in the day, but were only legends in the minds of black folks who saw them. These players never had an opportunity to rewrite history, nor would they be inducted into a hall of fame. They were captured in the memory banks of those who saw them and the Negro newspapers that wrote about them. Blacks and whites missed seeing the best athletes competing on a court, field or track until one day when a person said, "Something is missing; I just can't put my finger on it."

Just as a cake needs certain ingredients to make it whole, baseball, football, tennis, track and boxing took monumental steps in making the sports world's cake whole in the early to mid 1900s. In 1947, Jackie Robinson became the first black to enter the professional baseball ranks, Jack Johnson became the first black heavyweight champion in 1908, Jesse Owens shattered track and field records at the 1936 Olympics, and Althea Gibson became the first black to play in a U.S. Open final in 1958.

Once sports owners realized the best competition

came in all colors and there was money to be made by showcasing the best athletes, then and only then did the black athlete or minority athlete get the chance to display his or her skills.

Blacks have obliterated records set by other athletes and continue to defy the limits to what a body can do. Blacks continue to amaze people no matter what sport, and yet continue to be on the short end of the stick when all of the shattered records, high TV ratings, and record-setting attendances are transformed into money. Some people dismiss the success of black athletes and purport a theory that their bodies are made for these type of physical activities, not intellect, and that that's why they were ideal for slavery. But when you analyze the makeup of any sport, you will find that it takes more than an aggressive spirit or an ability to run or jump; it takes an intellectual ability as well to be successful. It takes determination, a competitive thought process, discipline to abide by rules and maintain shape and intellectual gamesmanship to win over a competitor; at the professional level, these are geniuses in their own right.

~The Next High School Wonder~

I can tell you that we have more black young men who want to play professional sports than they do any other profession. According to author G. Sailes, there is an overrepresentation of black males in particular sports and an under-representation in other segments of American society. He provides the example of percentages of black males competing in the NBA (77 percent), NFL (65 percent), MLB (15 percent), and MLS (16 percent) and contrasts them with the fact that fewer than 2 percent of doctors, lawyers, architects, college professors, or business executives are black males.

If you don't believe me, then come to a mentorship program and ask a group of ten young men ages ten to fifteen what they want to be. I'll bet you seven of them state they want to be professional athletes. Oh, and by the way, when you ask those seven if they play organized sports, at least three of the seven will tell you that they don't, but will next year.

So why are all these young men dreaming on something that only one in 22,000 will accomplish? Are the parents trying to live their dreams through their kids, or do the parents and children see sports as a possible way of becoming rich and famous? I saw firsthand when my children were playing recreational league sports that pushy parents transcended race, economic level, and social status. You've heard about the parents who get into fights with the coaches, players, and even officials over a game that is supposed to teach a youngster life lessons. This social trend has hurt a generation of kids, but has had a more devastating affect on black Americans. Let's examine the young men who want to play professional sports and, hopefully, you will get my point.

Many of the young men who visualize themselves

running a touchdown or slam-dunking a basketball make that dream a reality in their own minds. Many of these same kids don't and won't develop the talents to play at the varsity level; I think it can be worse for the young men who do have talent. They matriculate through elementary, middle, and high school holding out hope that something miraculous will happen to make them that blue chip player. They have no backup plan; if Kobe Bryant and Lebron James did it, then why not them? These same young men don't really apply themselves in school because they reason to themselves that reading, writing, and math aren't essential if they are going to get drafted. By the time the young men realize what has happened, they have placed all of their eggs in one basket and are halfway through high school with piss-poor grades and no alternative but a menial type job.

I know I have oversimplified this scenario, but I guarantee that if you were to follow the paths of some of the young men who plan to be professional athletes, you will find this to be hauntingly true.

~I Plan on Going Straight to the Pros~

If there is one sport that has helped perpetuate the cycle of uneducated and hopeless young black men, it's basketball. I used to think that no matter what your age, if you are talented enough to play at the professional level and receive the big bucks, then go for it. The whole purpose of going to school is to get that paper so that you can get a job and make money, right? Wrong. After doing some mentoring and personal observations, I decided that the NBA rule of accepting players right out of high school has caused more black males to be unprepared for the real world and increased their chances of living in poverty. (The NBA has now instituted a one-year removed from high school clause; it's a start, but I don't think that's good enough) Think about it: if you know you had to (1) be three years removed from high school as the NFL requires or (2) attend college to keep yourself proficient until you were eligible, then middle and high school take on a totally new meaning. Instead of those four or five young men stating they would go directly from high school to the professional ranks, they would be stating which college they were going to attend to showcase their talents.

By aspiring to attend college, people must make themselves academically eligible. And, attending college places people in a situation where they can learn a profession while pursing their athletic dream. If the athletic dream begins to dissipate, then they are already in the right setting for a different career. The person who is in college has a tremendous advantage over the person who is not in college; admission is half the battle, and once you are accepted and begin taking classes, then it's up to you and your finances to continue.

I don't have a problem with a young man aspiring to be a professional athlete. What I hate to see are the ones who don't have a backup plan. Many of us see how well

Lebron James and Kevin Garnett handle themselves on and off the court. These young men are great role models for any young man, but I will tell you that the two of them and a couple other seventeen- or eighteen-year-old phenoms are anomalies. Many of the instant pros suffer during their first few years, if they are lucky to still be around. Most are not ready to be instant millionaires, nor are they emotionally prepared for an adult life away from their support system. Many of those who strive to become pros without attending college are devastated emotionally and financially if they are not drafted. Financially? Yes, financially! If a high school player opts to enter into the NBA draft even after satisfying that first year from high school requirement, then he is automatically ineligible to play college basketball if he is not drafted. Those who are not eligible to be drafted and those who can't get into college for academic reasons try to keep proficient to win a basketball scholarship while others keep proficient for a shot at the draft. The more time you spend away from the public's eye, the less marketable you are. A year away from the public's eye can wipe away both college and professional aspirations. So yes, financially, a college degree gives you that edge and usually affords a higher-paying job.

At one point in my life, I thought that I wanted to be a professional football player. Then reality set in during my first season of college football. Fortunately, I had not placed my eggs in one basket. I have the following recommendations for parents who have young men that are up-and-coming stars:

1. Keep yourself grounded and don't see your kid as a lottery ticket. Many young men have been fooled into believing they are draft material by their parents, uncles, and friends. We sometimes place our kids on a higher pedestal than they should be.

2. Send your son to college, but seek a college that has a good graduation rate for its athletes and an administration that you feel will look out for his best interests.

3. Once your son is in college, check frequently on the progress of his academics. If he's not achieving, find out why through the coach and athletic department... that's part of their job.

4. Once your son is in college, if he is draft material, believe me, the pros will find you. Then it's your decision whether to enter him in the draft. If he is predicted to be a third-round or later draft pick, continue his education.

On the flip side of blaming the rules for our kid's disappointments and failures, we as blacks have to change our mind-set and de-emphasize the materialistic gains of a professional athlete. Although it can be very difficult, we need to conduct through our own media outlets a campaign that champions the honor of an education and professions other than sports. I know for a fact that through our mentorship program, we have inculcated in the minds of the kids who participate on a regular basis the importance of an education, specifically a college degree. I also know that we have swayed some who might have dreamt of becoming a professional athlete or some who had no clue on what they wanted to be to look deep inside themselves to identify their talents and match those up with an honorable profession. Through this constant reminding of education and strategic thinking, we now see more and more of our young men aspiring to do things that are well within their God-given talents.

I've had several young men who a year or two earlier would have stated... "a professional basketball player or professional football player" if they were asked what they wanted to be. These same young men now will tell you that they want to be a movie director, a teacher, a graphic artist, or zoologist. No longer do we have young men in our program who look down on professions that are not sports related. These young men now want to know about other careers than the ones they see on ESPN highlights. More importantly, we have them research their areas of interest to gain an understanding of what it takes to be successful in that field. The outcome is both astounding and tear making when you listen to them tell you what type of degree is necessary, which schools have the programs of their interest, and the gates one has to go through to become successful in that field.

If we as a people change our mind-set and look at the big picture—that the odds of finishing college and doing well for yourself are much greater than the one in 22,000 chance of becoming a professional athlete—then we will see more and more of our young men in the classroom and corporate offices and fewer and fewer on the streets and in jail.

~Pimps and Prostitutes~

If you think that is the main reason why I say "we just don't get it when it comes to sports," then you've missed the mark. Here is the reason we don't get it: college sports are probably the most exciting sporting venues you can watch on TV or attend in person. It's the amateur at his or her best, and you can always find an underdog that upsets the big dog. People who never attended college align themselves with the local or state college and are sometimes bigger supporters of the school than the alumni.

We tend to think of college athletics as a pure form of competition where athletes are giving their all for the love of their school and their sport. We listen to the announcers give the testimonies of the unfortunate young man or woman who overcame every imaginable obstacle to make it to the collegiate level and we think to ourselves, how wonderful that is. During football season, it's the Kick-off Classic and the bowl series that captivate our attention, and during basketball season it's March Madness that holds us hostage to our TVs. In America, we live, eat, and breathe sports, especially college sports. We watch the players coming out of the tunnel or locker room and imagine the lifestyle they must live. We imagine how it must feel to be on national TV and how it must feel to have your name called in front of thousands of spectators or see yourself on ESPN. We even wonder what's going through the mind of the draft prospects: Will they make it? Who will draft them? Where will they live? How will they spend the big bucks? What we rarely hear or ask is what is the graduation rate of these young men and women who play college sports. What's sad about student athletes is that only 27 percent of males and 35 percent of females actually complete four or five years and earn a degree. About 14 percent of black basketball players graduate from college.

If that is not a shock to you, then what I'm about to say may not be either. Sports for the black athlete is akin to prostitution, albeit a legal form of prostitution. The black athlete has to look at collegiate sports in that manner to maximize the benefits of its pimp *(college)*. The black athlete is courted by many pimps *(colleges)* to be a member of their stable; once the prostitute *(athlete)* determines who will treat him or her best, he or she accepts the terms of the pimp's *(college)* contract. The pimp *(college)* provides a free room; the best cuisine; travel throughout the nation; perks for close relatives; a chance to be recognized as the best prostitutes *(athletes)* around; and clientele *(fans)* who will love them, idolize them, and chastise them if they are not producing the kind of results desired.

The biggest benefit the pimp *(college)* promises to the prostitute *(athlete)* is an opportunity for four or sometimes five years to learn a different trade *(college degree)* so that he or she can become successful after his or her use as a prostitute *(athlete)* is gone. The pimp *(college)* will never promise the prostitute *(athlete)* the paper stating successful completion of trade skills *(college degree)* and will also hide the fact that if the prostitute *(athlete)* doesn't perform or gets into trouble, then all benefits *(continued education)* will be forfeited. If the prostitute *(athlete)* performs exceptionally well, then the prostitute *(athlete)* will be marketed for the folks *(pro recruiters)* who will pay for continued services, if the prostitute *(athlete)* performs well and does not get the paper *(college degree)*, then he or she will be marketed but if no pimps *(pro recruiters)* contract them for future services then they have no fall back plan however they will always be remembered as a good ho by the previous clientele *(fans)*.

The smart prostitutes *(athletes)* get that paper *(college degree)*, the really smart ones get two papers, one saying that they learned a trade and a second one saying that they mastered a trade *(masters degree)*. These type of prostitutes *(college graduates)* always come out ahead because they have a back up plan and if you don't watch out they will be the ones calling the shots. What I've seen over the years are a whole bunch of used-up prostitutes and ho's who have nothing to show but their memories. By no means am I trying to degrade the college athlete; I was a prostitute myself and a smart one. What I want to bring to light are the thousands of young men and women who missed the opportunity to get a degree and who have given their sweat, blood, and tears for institutions that benefit much more and usually don't care about them after the four years are up. Many times, the big colleges are the meanest, nastiest, ho-slapping pimps.

~Big Money in Sports~

Another reason why we just don't get it is because of the nearsightedness of our HBCU administrators. Most people think academics is the only pillar of success necessary to run/operate a competitive college. I'm certain that our HBCU administrators have been beaten up by newspapers, media, and others to increase their standards of admission or improve their facilities. With so much pressure to produce competitive students and improve the learning environment, the natural response is to focus solely on the academics aspect of the university to ensure they have good professors and a recruitment strategy.

One aspect that is quickly abandoned is the sports program and, in my humble opinion, the sports program is equally important as the academics. They go hand in hand to make a college/university viable. Think about it; most people want to associate with a winner, even the smart young men and women who may or may not have participated in a sport want to identify with a winner. You will have a large percentage of students who are attracted to a university solely because of the social aspects, and the sports program is an essential element of an attractive social scene. Not only are you able to recruit the more talented student and student athlete with a viable sports program, you are also able to generate millions of dollars to offset the operational costs of the college.

I know some of you think that the profits earned from the sports program stay in the athletic director's coffers; you can't be further from the truth. Those funds are used by the president and board of directors to build new science labs, hire top-notch professors, improve the campus grounds, fund research projects, and build new sports facilities. In 2002, the Southeastern Conference (SEC) distributed $79 million from TV income alone to the twelve schools in its conference, an average of $6.5 million per school. In recent years, total profits from the top fifty football programs amounted to $403 million, or an average of $8 million per school.

A few years ago, Penn State operated the fifth-largest football program in the nation, taking in $25.4 million in revenue. The program had expenses of $9.8 million. That's a surplus of nearly $15.6 million—a 61 percent margin. Ticket sales generated far and away most of that revenue: $15.7 million. Television and bowl-game income accounted for $5.6 million. Concessions brought in about $1 million. The rest came from corporate sponsorships, advertising, licensing royalties and program sales. The revenue figures don't include nearly $8.8 million that boosters and alumni paid to obtain season tickets. Including those donations, football accounted for a total of $32.4 million—82 percent of the athletic department's $42 million in revenue.

Sports fans why do you think we don't have a Division I football playoff? It certainly ain't the reason cited by the big university presidents: "a playoff will interfere with final exams." The reason we don't have a Division I playoff is because the bowl games are too lucrative to lose.

Bowl game earnings can be as little as half a million to as much as $12 million per school. If you add in the regular season football earnings, a top college program can sink another $5 million to $8 million more from ticket sales and corporate sponsorships into its bank accounts.

~The HBCU's Dilemma~

Football is the most lucrative of all sports for a college. The earnings from a college football program usually support many if not all of the other athletic sports. HBCUs unfortunately don't see the huge earnings that the top caliber football programs in country do. This can be attributed to many factors, but a couple that stand out are these programs' ability to draw corporate sponsorships and TV revenue. All HBCU football programs are in three of the four NCAA divisions: 1-AA, II, and III. None are in Division I. Division I schools are your big college schools such as Michigan, Texas, Miami, or even Wake Forest. These schools have strong alumni/fan support for their athletic programs, are able to raise money to logistically support the various teams and scholarships, and are regionally identifiable.

I stated "even Wake Forest" because admission into Division I college football has nothing to do with the size of the university. HBCUs such as Southern University, Howard University, and Florida A&M have twice and maybe three times the student population of Wake Forest.

Admission into Division I has to do with a school being able to support sixteen sports programs along with a great following from alumni/fans. As mentioned, Division I football programs are the only sports program that do not have a playoff type format to determine the national champion. However, Divisions I-AA, II, and III all have a football playoff. These playoffs do not draw large crowds; if televised at all, they are on the secondary channels of ESPN. There are very few sponsors and there are no big money payoffs. These playoffs are not tainted by the corporate sponsors. The players play to win a national title, and the alumni and fans love the playoffs because the best are selected to play for the title; there is no computer-generated formula to determine who plays and who doesn't.

Currently, only three of the four black conferences have teams that represent them in the playoffs. The South West Athletic Conference (SWAC) teams have opted out of the playoffs because the Bayou Classic and SWAC championship conflict with the start of I-AA playoffs. The dilemma for any of the conferences is, should the best team(s) of the conference play in a bowl game such as the Heritage or Pioneer Bowl or should it compete in the playoffs. Understandably, the Bayou Classic and SWAC championship generate a lot of money for the conference and schools; therefore, I don't blame them for opting out when the NCAA will not accommodate moving the start of the I-AA playoff by a week.

The "so what" is, that although the schools that

compete in the playoffs don't earn a lot of money, their programs gain regional and national exposure. Regional and national exposure makes it easier to recruit some of the top caliber players; players coming out of high school want to be on a winning team and certainly want to be able to compete for more than a conference championship, they want to compete for a national title. Top caliber athletes along with good coaching equates to competitive football, which ultimately results in good earnings from large crowds.

I'm all for the classics but am totally against the Black Bowl games that interfere with the playoffs. As a former football player, I would much rather have said that I made it to the playoffs or won a national championship than say my team won a bowl and was the black champion. Over the years, I've seen schools establish good football programs that compete in the NCAA playoffs and the results are incredible in terms of increased school spirit, alumni support, and recruiting of all students.

Another large source of revenue comes from the I-AA schools that are offered an opportunity to be a Division I's fodder. Some of the more competitive Division I schools have scheduled HBCU I-AA football programs during the beginning of the season to warm up and get the kinks out of their strategies before they play their conference schedule. The payment for a 1-AA school to play one of the top fifty programs could be as much as $500,000 for the team to show up; this amount in some cases is equal to ticket sales earnings for an entire season.

One of the biggest dilemmas for sports programs is to consider moving from Division I-AA to Division I. There are many naysayers out there that will tell you that the HBCU's sports programs need to remain in either I-AA or II/III until they can compete at Division I level or win a national title. I say exactly the opposite, if they meet certain requirements then they should move up. If a HBCU has the fan support as a Southern or South Carolina State and has the funding to adequately support sixteen programs, then it should move soon after developing a plan. Florida A&M competed in Division I in 2004, but met disaster because of issues within the program. There were many naysayers who got a vote of confidence with the failure of Florida A&M; however, if the school's house had been in order, these same naysayers would have been eating crow. With the right administration and athletic director/staff, a HBCU sports program can field teams that are competitive and economically viable. The only way we will be able to financially compete with the top caliber programs is for a HBCU to break the Division I barrier and become successful doing so.

Imagine some of the best athletes deciding to attend a HBCU... picture a small college campus with the bare necessities, a couple of dormitories, a dining facility shared by all, marginal to good professors, minimal resources to conduct research, minimal staff to operate the college, and no stadium. Given decent crowds, those top caliber athletes can transform a sports program and campus into a sprawling campus with abundant funds to upgrade staff, professors, and facilities within a few years. If you don't believe me, then go and ask the folks from Georgia Southern and Troy State. If the Jordan's, the Ruth's, the Lombardi's and the Gretzsky's built a house, then the Herschel Walkers and the Birds built universities.

Chapter IV:

Educational Meltdown

"The principle goal of education is to create men who are capable of doing new things, not simply of repeating what other generations have done—men who are creative, inventive and discoverers." Jean Piaget 1896-1980

~Understanding Why We Are Where We Are~

WHY DO SO many of our blacks not get the education they need to become successful in this society? Why don't we try harder to get across to our young boys and girls in grade school the importance of an education? How did we lose a large generation of black males? The answers to these questions come in various forms, but here are a few reasons why blacks, specifically black males, have not performed to their potential.

In the early 1900s, almost 90 percent of blacks still lived in the South. Around 1913, a series of events took place that devastated life and work for the black man and woman. The agricultural community was devastated from cotton's archenemy, the boll weevil, and the floods of Mississippi in 1915 disrupted and uprooted the lives of many blacks. These natural disasters along with the increase in lynching and Jim Crow discriminatory laws pushed blacks out of the South to the North and West Coast. At the same time, the effects of the American industrial revolution were in full force, and the demand for cheap labor could not be met by immigrants alone. Black workers became appealing for cheap unskilled labor in the Northern metropolitan areas.

The totality of these events became known as the Great Migration. By 1960, 40% of all Blacks lived outside the South, while 75% of all Blacks lived in cities. By transforming their rural southern backgrounds to fit their new urban homes, African Americans created a new Black culture. The factory jobs offered during this time required little or no formal education and, as a result, little emphasis was placed on education for the black man. Black women in the city were relegated to back-breaking service jobs as maids, cooks, and house cleaners. An education for a black woman meant access to clerical or office type work, and getting a formal education became a priority.

Blacks in the northern cities prospered with better paying jobs than would have been possible in the rural and urban areas in the South, Black communities in these cities were defined with a lower class, middle class and upper class that were no different from other minority and, in some cases, white communities. However, the gains of the civil rights movement had an impact on blacks throughout the country. The gains of the movement meant a playing field that was not quite level but that was at least conducive to play on. Blacks were now allowed to enter career fields from which they were once banned; blacks who had some supervisory responsibilities were now being recognized and compensated for their work. Educated blacks and those who prepared themselves for formal schooling had a great advantage over blacks who were uneducated and those who had not prepared themselves for formal schooling. The doors for better opportunity were cracked, and educated blacks got their foot in the door and earned skilled jobs such as teachers, professors, doctors, dentists, lawyers, bankers, managers, entrepreneurs, salesmen, skilled government positions, and the military officer ranks.

In return, these blacks sought the same things that whites always had: the house with the white picket fence and landscaped yards, schools and hospitals with great facilities, and access to the local social and community clubs. Then, another migration from the cities to the suburbs took place that sent the black middle class and wealthier blacks out of the well-structured inner-city communities to the suburbs. Along with the migration of people, many of the unskilled jobs in the cities began to dry up due to technological advances. Further complicating the situation, factories relocated to smaller cities and suburbs where environmental regulations were not as strict and unions were not as prevalent.

The migration of many of the educated blacks created

a void in these city communities and during the '70s and '80s, we had a large population of blacks living in and around a crumbling inner-city infrastructure. Many of the uneducated blacks were now unemployed. The disappearance of these jobs had a devastating impact on the families and individuals left in these communities.

A steady job provides structure and gives individuals and others a sense of purpose. "A child who grows up in a household where unemployment and irregular employment are the norm [does] not develop habits and behaviors that are necessary for success in the industrial economy. Such an environment is particularly harmful for males because unlike females, they have no major daily responsibilities for housework and childcare."

While many of the men who worked in factories lost their jobs, black women were either able to maintain employment or to find employment in the service industry. We began to see a shift in the black family structure from a two-parent home to a single parent shouldering the responsibility for the family. Many unemployed black men lost their self-esteem and self-worth, and some turned to drugs, alcohol, or crime to escape their plight. The community, now devoid of positive black male role models within the family and suffering from the exodus of the middle and upper class, witnessed young black males trying to learn on their own how to be men without any guidance or idea of how to do it. Black girls witnessed on a daily basis the work ethic of their mothers, and the importance of self-dependence and education.

Trapped in an inner city with no resources to get to the outside world, many black males were left to defend themselves and make a living anyway they could, hence the phrase "Trying to survive in the jungle." The quickest way to make money was through illegitimate measures. The payoff of an education was too far in the future.

~Knowing Where We Are Now~

Education is not just one of the factors for success; it is the main ingredient for success in today's society. The American society has transformed from an industrial to a consumer and service-based workforce. The blue-collar worker has been supplanted by the "no-collar" and white-collar workers. The no-collar workers are those who usually have little or no education. They are often immigrants who work for minimum or little more than minimum wage with little or no benefits. These are good, hard-working folks who have taken the menial jobs from the black and a few white workers; they are doing the jobs that blacks once had but then thought this line of work was beneath them. These folks now work at the chicken chain restaurants or convenience stores, are your maids at the hotels, and are doing jobs such as landscaping and construction. The skilled and unskilled jobs that paid well with good benefits have relocated to South America or Asia, where the labor is cheap.

The saying "you need to get an education" is more

relevant than ever. If you don't have a college degree or have a certified skill, then you are not competitive in today's workforce. Bottom line, there are few jobs around these days that require only a high school diploma that pay well with benefits for folks of any color. The good jobs at Firestones and Procter & Gamble in my hometown are rare these days. These plants have relocated or will eventually relocate to other parts of the world to become more profitable, or have streamlined the assembly line with new technology, essentially reducing or eliminating the number of unskilled jobs required.

~The Great Divide in Our Educational System~

So much to do has been made of the U.S. educational system from the politician to the parent. People seeking office will always spout out their concerns about the educational system and what must be done to fix it. They talk about more money to improve facilities and more money to raise test scores and sometimes even talk about more pay for teachers.

When couples/families relocate, they often look for the so-called "good school districts." I have always been puzzled when I hear the good school districts; exactly what makes a school district good? Could it be test scores, placement to college, better facilities, better teachers, a diverse school, graduation rates, or school colors… exactly what is it? I sure would like to know the winning formula. I'm not an educator myself but through my own children and mentoring at various schools I would say for that schools in the suburbs away from the inner city are generally the same. There is a great divide between the inner-city, suburban, and in some cases the rural schools. The great divide is based on a number of factors ranging from lack of funding to improve facilities to lack of certified teachers to expectations of the student from the community/parents to parental involvement. I would like to focus on these four factors because in my mind's eye they seem to be the root of the problems we face in the education system.

Having the right environment goes a long way in helping a child learn. Statistics show that a nourished child in a comfortable setting will do much better than one who is hungry or in an extreme cold or hot setting; there are just too many competing personal needs to learn.

Many of the metropolitan cities have schools that just don't have the right learning environment. The city of Atlanta has just such a school, where I spent at least two hours each week mentoring young men and women. Before I began mentoring at the school, I was required to attend a seminar and was cautioned along with other prospective mentors about the condition of the schools and the hardships many of these kids faced. The seminar speaker, a past superintendent, gave us a heart-wrenching talk about his experiences as a principal in an inner-city school. He told us that many of the kids started their morning between 4:30 and 5:00 a.m., getting themselves up, dressing themselves, and walking to the nearest bus or rail station. They would ride to the point where they would be picked up by the public school bus and then be ferried to school, for some a two-hour journey. The gentlemen stated that these kids did this routine, rain or shine. To acknowledge their desire to be at school, he and his staff would form a victory line each morning and applaud as the kids filed into school. How do you expect a child to learn if he or she had to make a two-hour journey each day and oh, by the way, didn't even eat until arriving at school.

The former superintendent went on to say that his school and many others had inferior facilities and lacked the technological resources such as computers and lab equipment to enhance learning. He had a group of students who participated in an enrichment program at one of the newly built suburban schools. After entering this new facility, his students felt angry, jealous, and ashamed of their learning environment. One student noticed that the suburban school even had a washer/dryer along with a pantry full of school T-shirts to give to students during rainy days when they got wet coming to school.

During my two years of mentoring at that school, I was amazed at the inferior facilities for these inner-city schools. Things that were common when I was in high school over twenty years ago were absent at this school. Some of the bathrooms were locked and others were in such horrible condition, the grounds weren't kept, old style desks and a few new desks intermingled in the classrooms, the computers were obsolete, walls had not been painted in years, beverage machines were inoperable or had bars placed on them, classrooms were too hot or too cold.

This is no different from a school system in East St. Louis where, on occasion a school closes due to sewage backups in the kitchen. Teachers have little chalk or paper to provide students and receive modest salaries. Only 55 percent of students graduate; 20 percent of those who graduate go on to college. Chemical plants and toxic waste incineration factories surround the schools. Schools have a ninety-nine percent segregation rate. Thirty students sit in a classroom designed to hold fifteen. Textbooks have been around for twenty years. In the best school in the system, a trip to the bathroom proves quite revealing. Most toilets do not function. Toilets do not have seats. Nowhere to be found are paper towels, soap or toilet paper.

Even a child will know his or her value to society by the size of investment into the facilities and places where he or she lives, learns, and plays.

I know that the tax base in an area determines the type of resources available to build or improve a school. But I also know there are billions of dollars allocated for the defense of this country and billions of dollars that are allocated for subsidies that could go a long way in eliminating the lack of facilities. There have been many proposals on how to ensure equal facilities for all schools; some suggest vouchers, others suggest special schools or busing, and some have even suggested spreading the tax revenue as a remedy.

Although school funding varies among states, I truly believe there should be some parameters established by either the national or state governments to ensure there is a minimum criteria met for school facilities. Realistically, I know that we will not see a national standard, but what I propose is for each state to develop minimum criteria for school facilities. These criteria should address obsolescence of computers, textbooks, and lab equipment. They should address standards for bathrooms, recreation, and eating facilities or outlets. Lastly, they should address the number of teachers and staff required to maintain a proper learning environment. How would this be funded? I would tax a percentage of the wealthy and middle-income school districts to subsidize the costs to maintain the minimum criteria. If a state has a lottery, the winners would be taxed to ensure the standards are met and maintained. Lastly, I would form an independent board of parents, former teachers, and business leaders to monitor spending and ensure standards are met.

One researcher found that low socioeconomic status (SES) students often find themselves at another disadvantage not of their own making:

They generally are clustered in schools that are grossly under funded, while other nearby schools attended primarily by higher SES students receive substantially more funding on a per-pupil basis. Although the relationship between higher levels of per-pupil expenditures and improved levels of academic performance is not clear cut… researchers have continued to press the case that inequities unfairly penalize those living in poor school districts. One recent study used new cost-analysis models to review spending patterns in eighty-four academic high schools in New York. For each additional $100 spent on classroom instruction, students gained as much as 18 points on the combined scores for the mathematics and verbal sections of the Scholastic Aptitude Tests after adjustments were made for student socioeconomic status and teaching experience of school staff... Some policy makers now argue that financial restructuring must take place to help low-SES students overcome the disadvantages built into current school finance structures... It seems self-evident that if poor children attend poorly funded schools, they are not likely to achieve at the same levels as their counterparts attending better funded schools." There should be no reason in this great country to have such inequalities in the places that our children learn.

The next factors span across all socioeconomic layers. Teachers are teachers, not doctors, nurses, policeman, psychologist, or physicians. Teachers ought to be role models and good citizens, but we have come to expect too much out of them. Policemen have become fixtures in the schools, along with day care centers for the teenager who gave birth during the school term and alternative schools for those kids who really just need a good ass whippin' (excuse me). Parental involvement is slowly giving way to the school and all the expectations we place on it. We even try to make an excuse that since children are at school most of the day and year, the school has the major role in their upbringing. That's why we have a need for the day care centers, psychiatrists, social workers, and police in the school.

I hear teachers all the time complain about the lack of parental involvement and when they recommend Ole Johnny for suspension then you better believe his mom is coming to school to raise holy hell because Johnny would never curse at a teacher. Johnny doesn't curse at home so why would he do it at school? More than likely it ain't the first time Johnny's been in trouble; it's just that if Johnny is suspended, then Mom has to make arrangements to watch or baby sit him. Oh, by the way, that's probably the first time the parent has communicated with the teacher or school administration. In many instances the parents don't show up to PTA, they don't establish communication with the teachers, and they don't know the child's progress in class.

Now, we can't always blame the parents; some of the blame can be cast toward lack of certified teachers. This is the direct result of an antiquated system to recruit teachers and teacher pay. There is a common perception that teachers are not really in the professional ranks and therefore should not be paid as much as accountants or lawyers. Some will even argue that all you have to do to become a teacher is to graduate from college and regurgitate the information you learned while in college. In essence, there is no skill associated with teaching; you see no tangible results from teaching as you would from an architect who designs a building for people to see and use.

There are no immediate impacts on life in the manner of doctors. Further exacerbating this issue is the fact that the National Education Association reports that the teaching field is comprised mostly of women, 79 percent, which commonly leads to inequities of pay. Lastly, since teachers only work a nine-month schedule and are off during most federal holidays, why in the world should they receive more pay or be paid comparable to other professional ranks that work year-round?

This type of mind-set and the traditional thinking of using teaching colleges as the sole source for growing teachers has stymied the teacher growth needed to properly educate our children. The traditional ways of growing teachers required a person to graduate from college with a teaching degree, then take a certification test.

In the past, college graduates who did not matriculate through the education curriculum were not heavily recruited. No provisions were made to allow their experiences in the corporate or military fields to substitute for portions of the certification necessary to become a teacher.

As noted in a U.S. House Education and Workforce Committee report on certification, former Education Secretary Rod Paige in 2003 "joined a rebellion against sole reliance on traditional teacher certification, saying teaching colleges should no longer have a monopoly over who is qualified to educate children." Secretary Paige endorsed the new American Board for Teacher Certification of Teacher Excellence, whose mission is to certify subject experts, experienced professionals, and military veterans as public school teachers even if they don't have degrees in education.

Teacher certification is necessary and the lack of 100 percent certified teachers in a school can be one of the factors for some schools' dismal test performance scores. We certainly don't want people with no background or experience in special education or physics or even history teaching our children. However, relying on the teaching colleges to produce the number of teachers required and the recruiting methods used in the past to draw folks with real bona fide experience to the teaching arena has proven ineffective.

Another reason why we don't have a large selection of teachers is pay. Most people will agree that teachers are underpaid for the work and results they produce. The NEA reported that the average contract salary for teachers in 2001 was $43,262 for approximately fourteen years of tenure. Although this may seem all right for a nine-month year, when you compare this to other professions' pay, teachers lag significantly behind. "Between 1994 and 2004, the economy has grown 16 percent on a real capita basis, but teacher pay has grown just 2.2 percent. The economy is growing at almost eight times the rate of teacher pay."

Think about it: if it weren't for our teachers we wouldn't have the doctors, lawyers, architects, or any of the other higher-paying professions. Understanding why we have a shortage of certified teachers needs to be examined, and my thoughts go something like this: The teaching profession in the past has not effectively developed a national plan to aggressively recruit folks to teach. I look at what the military did to recruit its officers after it went to an all-volunteer force, sometime after the Vietnam War. The U.S. Army had significant problems recruiting young men and women in its volunteer force, especially officers. As a result, the Army attracted many young men and women through its Reserve Officer Training Corps (R.O.T.C.) with full and partial scholarships, free textbooks, and a monthly stipend. The military made the pay more competitive. Combined with the medical and dental benefits, the total package for an officer in many cases outmatched the packages offered in the corporate world. The pool of folks joining R.O.T.C. increased significantly and the military was able to pick the cream of crop for its most deployed forces.

Along with the pay increases, the Army and other services put on a huge marketing campaign to attract prospective officers and restore the value of serving the country. This campaign propelled the military's image as not only honorable but as one of the best professions to be associated with. I know there are some incentives to recruit teachers, but don't think that these campaigns have had national appeal, nor have the recruiting methods had any grip/teeth.

We need a recruiting and marketing campaign that is focused on a couple of key areas. One would be to allure more males and minorities to the teaching field.

According to a NEA study in 2003, men comprise only 21 percent of the teaching force, and African Americans comprise only 6 percent. The image of teaching needs to be addressed in this campaign so that folks outside of the profession will respect this career field. This campaign should focus on the contribution to society that teachers make. For many of us, the impact that teachers make to our society just doesn't register. We all know about the impacts that scientists, doctors, or even entertainers have on our society, but seldom do we make a big deal about the contributions that our teachers make on a daily basis.

I would name my national recruiting program the Future Teacher Cadre Program (FTCP), and have regional districts responsible for recruiting the top students emerging from high school and the top students in college. These efforts would focus heavily on males and minorities until a proportionate balance is achieved. The program would award partial and full scholarships to include textbooks, a monthly stipend, and a laptop computer. Even those who did not win scholarships but participated in this program would receive a monthly stipend if they maintained a certain grade point average. The students who completed the program would receive a letter of recommendation from the regional director and placement advisers would assist them in finding positions.

Completion of this program would require a three- or four-year commitment within the regional district or repayment of all scholarship funding. Along with the FTCP, the marketing campaign would be an essential element in expanding the pool of teachers and educating the public on the profession of teaching. The marketing campaign would be similar to the Marine and Army commercials that go a long way in telling the story of the nobility, service, and compensation to those who enter. We need to nationalize a program with appropriate funding and hold folks responsible for ensuring we have schools that can pick the brightest and best teachers.

~Integration, the Double-Edged Sword~

What has integration done for us lately? Integration has helped the plight of minorities in tremendous ways, and I'm grateful for the folks who sacrificed themselves to make this a reality. But if there is one area of integration that hurt the black race, it is education. Before and during the civil rights era, we as a people didn't have the resources nor was "separate but equal" equal. But we sure had the desire to learn and bring the best out of one another.

During those times, you didn't have many discipline problems. If a boy or girl slumped down in his or her chair or talked out of place, then he or she didn't get written up or sent to the principal. The child received discipline, a slap across the back of the head or a paddling in the palm of the hand or a good twist of the ear. Heck, sometimes a nasty look or good chewing-out in front of the classmates would correct the problem. If that didn't work, the talk of working in the fields all day as an alternative did. I vividly remember a junior high school assistant principal who was a former professional baseball pitcher giving me three of his best swings from his paddle for misconduct in class. That was the last time I acted up in class. I also recall an English teacher who summoned the football coach to come and discipline one of the players for talking out of place during class. Coach heard the announcement over the intercom and was there within minutes. He took the kid out of class and when the kid came back into class, he didn't say another word out of turn... his butt was too sore to even think about speaking out again.

We have allowed ourselves to buy into the notion that what is good for the majority is good for us. Any parent who has two or more children will tell you that each child is different and what may stimulate one won't necessarily stimulate another. Successful parents understand this and apply their discipline, rewards, and even love according to the child's temperament. I will use this as an analogy to the situation of blacks because we know or knew what worked for our children; time out, stand in the corner, and demerits just don't work for us. Don't tell me we are all the same because we are not; we acknowledge differences in almost everything that affects us. We do better in the sun than other folk of lighter hue and our body makeup is more susceptible to certain diseases while others are prone to different ones. So why can't we see that there are differences in the way that we discipline and learn?

Am I saying that we should have a separate curriculum? No, what I am saying is that we need to acknowledge that the way we used to discipline worked and restore that type of discipline back in the school system. What we need are black males to give back by entering the education field to restore discipline and set an example for many of our misguided young men.

Black females are three times more likely than black males to attain a college degree. Why is this? One of the reasons is that there exists this phenomenon within our ranks of young black boys that if they do well in school, then they are trying to be white. When I polled the young men in my mentorship program, almost all of them either had someone tell them that or subscribed to that theory.

This belief is being voiced in epidemic proportions and I believe this hippty hop/gangsta rap music further exacerbated the problem. When you think a boy with gold teeth and oversized pants walking around as if he just had a bowel movement in his pants, speaking a language neither he nor anyone else understands is who you want to be like, then school and the work and rules that go along with it just ain't that appealing.

Secondly, the black male, especially an educated one has always been a perceived threat to others. Because of the negative news coverage of blacks, many whites (not necessarily intentionally) write off many black boys or lower their expectations of their learning ability. Here is a statistic to bring you to reality: black children represent 17 percent of the public school population nationwide, but 41 percent of all children in special education; of that 41 percent, 85 percent are black males. I know teachers have a tendency to write off black males, not necessarily because they want to place the children at a disadvantage but mainly because they don't understand and bring their mental stereotypes to the job.

I guarantee you that half of that 41 percent shouldn't be in special education; however, if you have no advocate for the child, then he will remain there. As long as the black boy behaves in class and causes no distraction to others, whatever he does as far as his class work is gravy. Heck, as long as the boy passes, that's one less parent to deal with. So, as this well-mannered boy matriculates through school, he is neither encouraged nor pushed to his potential. By the time he's finished with high school, he has only a few prospects of going to college and more than likely he will only qualify for a tech school.

For whatever reason, so many young black boys are passed from one grade to another and essentially cycled right out of school. I have to reiterate to my son all of the time that his goal is to finish college, not just high school. Depending on the school district and location, you may or may not hear young boys and girls talking about college. At many of the predominately black schools, you will rarely hear kids talking about which college they will attend. This is a total contrast to the more affluent school districts where kids not only talk about which college they will attend but will "dis" a college that they perceive to be inferior to the one they chose.

The media has done a dandy trick little trick by playing on the sympathy of the public and making excuses for our inability to keep pace with the educational statistics of other races. Some people in the professional field will say that 200 years of slavery is still affecting the current generation; others have published articles and books that analyze the head size and brain weight to determine who is more likely to be smart. Some have just plain out said we don't have the capacity to learn as quickly as others. We too have bought into this concept; do you remember Ebonics, the black language of the inner city? What in the world were we thinking when we introduced this as an alternative language? It was just another excuse to cover up the lack of emphasis we have placed on education.

We have allowed ourselves to buy into the miss-theory that we cannot achieve in the fields of science, math, engineering, and technologies and I too was one who followed the path of least resistance and focused on a general relatively easy field. I repeat: what you see the most is what you strive to be. Why are our folks so much more susceptible to being caught up in a reality for a few when others see the boundless opportunities for many?

~The Band-Aid Approach to Remedy the Great Divide~

Vouchers are championed by many politicians as the savior for parents who want to get their children out of schools with substandard test scores or who want to place their children in a better learning environment. But the truth of the matter is that vouchers won't help the number of folks cited in the studies and reports. In reality, vouchers will only subsidize the private education of those who are already in a decent school district or help those get out of a school district whose demographics have changed.

I'm a critic of wholesale issuance of vouchers, because most voucher plans don't cover the complete cost of tuition for a school and even if they did, then a poor family would have to pay for transportation and other extracurricular expenses incurred to satisfy school requirements. Additionally, if the voucher covered partial or full tuition, then what guarantee is there that a child will be enrolled in the parent's choice of school? Most private schools have a waiting list, and a large percentage of public schools, especially the ones considered good schools, are overcrowded with more and more families moving to that area so their children can attend the schools.

If you had a situation in which kids had to get on a waiting list for a private or public school, what would be the criteria for getting on the list? I can guarantee you the criteria won't be weighted in favor of the lower-income family. I do think that in certain situations that vouchers can work, but they are only a work-around to the real issues that face our education system. Once the real issues that face our educational system—restoring discipline in our schools; restoring the principles of reading, writing, arithmetic, and science; increasing teacher pay; offering incentives to draw more qualified teachers in the workforce; and increasing parent involvement—are addressed, we won't have to worry about vouchers and other workarounds.

~Changing Mind-sets~

Many of us who are parents need to take personal inventory of our priorities and place the education of our children as the number one priority. Many of our black parents will not attend a parent-teacher conference, PTA meeting or open house. However, we will make time for a sporting event, a TV show, a concert, or a play.

I know that many of our black parents who are not able to make it to the school are working two or three jobs to maintain a comfortable life for themselves and their children. I also know that if we sacrifice our time to have a certain lifestyle, other aspects of our life may come back to haunt us in the long term. Just as the minister says, "If you can jump up and down and cheer for a football team then you should have the same enthusiasm when you come to the house of worship," I say that we as parents should place the same emphasis, energy, and enthusiasm on academics as we do for the soccer team, basketball team, AAU teams, cheerleading squad, step team, football team, gymnastics, swimming team, or beauty pageant. You've seen the parent or parents who are intimately involved in every aspect of their child's extracurricular activities; they attend every game, every practice, keep statistics on the players, and volunteer for almost any and everything related to the activity.

Although this is the extreme situation, many of us devote a lot of our time and will even leave work early to ensure our child gets to the recital, practice, or game on time. But we will rarely take off to ensure we meet with the teachers or attend an open house on a regular basis.

When I was stationed in Mississippi, my wife taught at a local high school that was predominately black. She might have one or two parents out of a possible 120 who would visit her room during an open house or PTA meeting; however, at the home and away football games, you could count on at least 20 percent of the parents, cheering for their child or as spectators. What's wrong with this picture? I can tell you that sports and any other activity that highlights our children's talents are a lot more appealing than discussing the progress of our child's learning. Seeing them participate is visual. Receiving a progress report or final grade or even chatting with a teacher is more personal and does not lend itself to the same type of exposure and recognition.

For some of our parents, there is an inhibition to attend an academic event because they may be intimidated by the teacher or may not want to hear any bad news about their child. Some even think of going to a school to talk with an administrator in the way they think of visiting the doctor or hospital, and for most of us that means there will always be some bad news or warnings involved. So, they avoid those institutions unless absolutely necessary, such as when there is a threat of suspension or failure.

Here is a proposal on how we change this mind-set: first, the parent has to be willing to meet the administration a part of the way, if not halfway. More importantly, the school administration has to do a better job of marketing the academic success of their kids and value academics over extracurricular activities. The key to getting to the parent is through the child.

If I were a high school principal, I would elevate my academic stars as much as I would a state championship football team. I would identify those students who performed exceptionally well in the classroom on a consistent basis to form an academic team; just as you do for any other sport. I would hold a special pep rally just for my academic team, with the band and cheerleaders, and introduce them just as you do the starting lineup for a basketball game and then parade them around. I would challenge other students to become a part of the team and list the criteria for the team. At the home football, baseball, and basketball games I would have the announcer recognize either the academic team or members of the academic team before they introduced the starting lineup for the sports team. The same would apply for any other pep rallies held; the academic team would be introduced first before the players of that sport. The academic team would receive letter jackets with special recognition just as the sports programs do.

Another proposal to break the barrier is to ask the parents' employers to provide paid absence of no more than three hours to attend an open house or PTA meeting during normal work hours.

These are just a couple of my simple ideas that may or may not have been explored. But I know that we have to continue to try innovative approaches to get our parents involved as well as send a message to our kids that academics is most important.

Chapter V

Remove the Log in Your Eye before You Criticize the Splinter in Someone Else's Eye

"Honest criticism is hard to take, particularly from a relative, a friend, an acquaintance or a stranger."
Franklin P. Jones

I WANT TO start off this chapter by acknowledging that I'm far from perfect and have been a bit hypocritical myself over the course of my life. However, I think I've stayed within the mainstay of human boundaries. If you would, please give me a pass on my life and focus on what I'm saying. I want to hone in on a couple of controversial topics that blacks don't like to discuss in public and certainly don't want anyone else to bring up. These topics are discussed when it's only us. I want to talk about them because I can, because only a few will, and because I care.

~I Want my 40 Acres and a Mule~

How do you make things right for a group of folks who were enslaved for generation after generation? How do they earn a living once you decide to free them, and how do you expect them to survive in your society if you banned them from learning how to read and write? If you brainwashed them to believe they had no history and you had your most moral authorities preach to them that they were less than human, how do you expect them to lift up their heads with pride and confidence?

I have never been a big supporter of reparations but after researching this piece, I believe that something should have been done many, many decades ago to right the wrongs of slavery in this country. One thing that needs to be changed right away is to record in our schoolbooks the many accomplishments of all Americans. It's absolutely mind-boggling to discover the many accomplishments by blacks and other races that you don't hear about unless you dig deep in the libraries or have someone pass on to you their contributions.

When I saw the HBO movie *Something the Lord Made* recently, I came to tears watching the determination, strength, brilliance, humility, and commitment of Vivien Thomas, who almost single-handedly developed a procedure to correct heart defects in children. The amazing thing about this story is that Vivien had no prior medical experience nor had he attended college. When he developed this process, it was taboo to operate on the human heart. This procedure changed the course of medicine and undoubtedly saved millions of folks who would have otherwise died.

History is so important for all races. Jews understand this and will never let you forget the genocide and concentration camps during World War II, nor should they. Even though there are volumes of records that Jews were persecuted during this period, there are a significant number of Germans, Arabs, and Klansmen who will tell you in a minute that there were no such things as concentration camps or ovens to burn bodies. If they continue to push this propaganda, over time people who do not research history will come to believe that the Jews were just embellishing or even lying about their history. I saw the ovens and the concentration camps, and I'm a true believer that the survivors endured hell on earth.

When it comes to blacks and our decades of suffering, folks of other races say that slavery and lynching occurred way before your generation and some of these atrocities even occurred before your parents' generation, so why do you blacks always bring up the past and talk about this nonsense of reparations? I will tell you that it's important to know your past, and the pain is still there when you read about the atrocities, hear about them from your parents or grandparents, see pictures or have been unfortunate enough to have witnessed them.

I don't ever want to diminish what blacks, Jews, Native Americans or any race went through during periods of oppression. These periods have everlasting effects that are passed from one generation to another. What is somewhat unique about the African American struggle is the fact that in recent history, other races were compensated in some fashion for their ordeals while African Americans weren't.

The Jews were monetarily compensated by the Germans. We even compensated the Japanese by rebuilding Japan even though they bombed Pearl Harbor and committed just as many horrific acts to the Chinese as did the Germans to the Jews. We compensated Native Americans by giving them back a portion of their own land along with a tax break for gambling on their reservations. The closest thing to reparations for African Americans was the promise of "forty acres and a mule" by a few generous white men who wanted to right a few wrongs of slavery.

Forty acres and a mule resulted from General William T. Sherman's march to the sea and Secretary of War Edwin M. Stanton's stance to compensate the newly freed men. These gentlemen met with twenty black community leaders of Savannah, Georgia, in early January 1865. On January 16, 1865, General Sherman issued a special order, Field Order #15, setting aside the Sea Islands and a thirty-mile inland tract along the southern coast of Charleston for the exclusive settlement of blacks. Each black family would receive forty acres and a mule to work the land.

Here is a summary of Special Field Orders, No. 15, Headquarters Military Division of the Mississippi, 16 January 1865. Orders & Circulars, serial, 44, Adjutant

General's Office, Record Group 94, National Archives:

General Rufus Saxton was assigned by Sherman to implement the Order. On a national level, this and other land, confiscated and abandoned, became the jurisdiction of the Freedman's Bureau, which was head by General Oliver Otis Howard (Howard University). In his words he wanted to… give the freedmen protection, land and schools as far and as fast as he can. However, during the summer and fall of 1865, President Johnson issued special pardons, returning the property to the ex-Confederates. Howard issued Circular 13, giving 40 acres as quickly as possible. Upon his knowledge, Johnson ordered Howard to issue Circular 15, returning the land to the ex-Confederates.

So when do blacks finally receive their forty acres and a mule? Never. It will be a cold day in hell before blacks receive any type of reparations. My personal view is that a couple of things need to take place if we don't receive monetary reparations. First, Congress needs to establish an atonement commission to study the effects of slavery, develop strategies to close the racial divide, and assist in rewriting our history. Second, we need to make the Fourth Amendment in the 1965 Voting Rights Act permanent. The Fourth Amendment was a temporary measure to remove all of the unlawful prerequisites and voting obstacles placed in front of minority voters. This mandate should cover all of the fifty states, not just the ones identified in the initial amendment and subsequent updates.

There have been many prominent folks who've thrown

out ideas on reparations. Even Republican Alan Keyes recommends making a generation of blacks tax free. Many of the black organizations support reparations as well, but how such a program would be administered if granted is very unclear. Representative John Conyers has been trying for the last fifteen or so years to get a bill passed that would establish a commission to examine slavery and its effects on blacks and America. His commission would be comprised of legal experts, economists, historians, genealogists, and others and would hold hearings across the country. However, a man of his influence and statue can't even get the bill debated in Congress.

If hell freezes over and we do receive reparations, I recommend the funding be evenly distributed to the Historically Black Colleges and Universities for full-ride scholarships of deserving young men and women, specifically those living in the inner cities. I think the bus has passed us by on our fight for reparations; we should have received them but we didn't. Now, the time has come that we must at least ensure whatever rights our ancestors fought for are maintained and that we gain momentum in our efforts to level life's playing field.

~Always a Victim~

Some of our so called leaders have bought into the notion that the current plight of our race is due solely to decades of slavery, Jim Crow laws, lynching, and segregation. They constantly look to the government as the sole source to cure our problems and rarely speak out against issues that we can remedy ourselves. I call this state of being Victimology. 1.a. The constant state of a person or group of people who feel they are victims even when they cause harm or injury to themselves. 2.a. A person or group of people who blame any misfortune on another person or group of people.

There is a tendency in both the white and black cultures to view blacks as victims and this tendency usually relates to one historic event, slavery. It is part of the coexistence of white and black cultures; the two cultures are dissimilar, but need each other, and the notion is asserted by whites and internalized and acted out by blacks that black suffering is authentic and black success is selling out.

This constant beat of victimization has created a sense of apathy in the white community. Whites would rather not address a black issue for fear of being labeled a racist, and in the black community you have some people who deeply believe low achievement and the current plight of blacks is solely the result of being a victim in a racist society. If children are told daily that they can be successful, they will eventually believe it. The same applies if you're told daily that you are victim of "the man"; you will believe it and live it.

What's hard to grapple with as a black male is the apathy shown not by whites but by other blacks who are in a position to help but do absolutely nothing. I know that there are many blacks who are doing wonderful things in their community to try and uplift others but compared with the magnitude of issues and numbers of folks who need help it almost seems nonexistent. It becomes so frustrating, hearing about the issues, crime, or comparison statistics from the news outlets, TV programs, and radio.

Sometimes I just don't understand. I understand that black men and women were beaten and even killed when they tried to read and write, but don't understand why we now have to beat our kids to learn at school. I understand that black men and women sang spirituals in the cotton fields to praise their God and make time go by, but don't understand why we now degrade our women and praise killing through our rap music. I understand that black women were raped by white slave owners and treated like the scum of the earth, but don't understand why black men now impregnate our black women and leave them to fend for themselves. I understand that black men and women were promised by the government forty acres and a mule and didn't get it, but don't understand why we now are more concerned about the mule (car) than the acres (property). I understand that everyone had to pull his or her own weight to survive and that we took pride in what we did no matter how menial the task, but I don't understand why we now expect someone else to help us carry our load and frown at work that we think is beneath us. I understand that black men were lynched for looking at a white woman or for being too proud or perceived as an economic threat, but don't understand why black men now will kill other black men over a pair of tennis shoes or because of the color of a shirt.

Why did we get so upset when Bill Cosby told us we need to clean up our backyards before we start blaming others for our problems? I thought it was absolutely refreshing to hear one of us admonish us. I get so tired of hearing the professors of Victimology preaching their doctrine. They say it's not our fault because we are still adjusting from slavery and the civil rights era. They say that we need more government programs to help us over the hump and they say that the government and law officials should stop targeting us. Yet when we had the epidemic of black on black crime, the crack addiction among our folks in the inner city, the phase of carjacking and now the large population of young black men who await the fast life of money opposed to working a legitimate job, these professors of Victimology were and are no where to be found to chastise or admonish others about these destructive lifestyles. But let someone of a different race make a comment, no matter how true, and then the professors will quickly don their Victimology robes and scream foul to every camera and microphone available. Heck, they will even organize a march or protest against the individual; just ask the Mexican president, who stated that Mexicans will do the work that Blacks won't.

I'm not trying to make light of our problems, and I know that police brutality and other injustices exist. When we have situations such as we had in Columbus, Georgia, in 2004 where we had a forty-year-old model citizen and executive of an insurance company get pulled over in a SUV with his friends by a rogue cop and shot in the head without any provocation, then I'm all about marching and protesting. The black officers in the Army all know that if they violate the Military Code of Justice, they will be disciplined more harshly than others. That's a given and we even talk about it. The difference is that those officers understand it and, for the most part, they stay away from the things that will warrant discipline. We as a people know that, so why in the heck don't we heed the many lessons learned from the dead and the many brothers and sisters in jail?

Another thing: why in the world do we want to tear up or burn our own neighborhood when there is an injustice? Who in the hell do you think we're hurting! During the LA riots, we were the stupid ones, breaking into shops, stealing TVs, burning down the grocery stores that we patronize on the first of the month, wrecking the barber and beauty shops that we frequent on a weekly basis, and burning down the Korean corner stores where we cashed our checks. Do you think the outside world gave a damn? Nope, because they ensured the mayhem was confined in the black neighborhoods. If we had that much energy to tote a TV and washing machine on our shoulders, throw a brick through a window, and gather material to set a building ablaze then we ought to have enough freakin' energy to get off of our butts and learn a trade so that we can make a difference.

During my stay in Washington, D.C., a senseless

murder occurred almost every month. Young people were killed by stray bullets from drive by shootings or by carjackers losing control of cars, yet there were no marches or admonishments by the professors of Victimology. There were a few courageous individuals who spoke out against these senseless killings; however, there were too many of the professors-in-training calling on the government to do something.

I know one person of inner city clout who will be speaking out more and that's former Washington Mayor Marion Barry, who was robbed at gunpoint in January 2006 by two young thugs. Out of all the people in D.C. to rob, they chose the man who has always been an advocate for the poor and those who have hit hard times. I would think he would be the least likely candidate for a robbery. Many folks come up to the former mayor and pay their respects by greeting him, and some request favors from him. On this wintry evening, two young men befriended the former mayor by carrying his groceries to his apartment. He allowed the thugs entrance into his home and paid them a few dollars for their effort. The young thugs departed his home, came back later, robbed him at gunpoint, and then fled the scene.

The true tragedy of this incident is not that the former mayor felt betrayed or that he was put into harm's way but his remarks to the media. He said he did not want to prosecute these two thugs; he just wanted them to turn themselves in. When I heard that comment, I immediately thought that he had a substance relapse and was on the pipe again. You know as well as I do that it will be a cold day in hell when those two hoodlums turn themselves in.

Marion Barry's remarks send a message to the thug community that it's OK to rob someone, especially a black person, because we believe in love, not tough love. I'm sure he rationalized that they were victims of this racist society and if in a better situation wouldn't have threatened him. He bought into the Victimology theory and look how he responded to the threat on his life; no one deserves to be physically threatened without punishment no matter if you're black, white, red, or green. When we as leaders look the other way or don't directly take on issues that face our community, we will eventually become victims ourselves.

I now call upon the few brothers and sisters who really care about our plight and are not concerned with name recognition or glory to denounce the professors of Victimology. We as a people ordain you to replace these fakes and shakedown artists and take the rightful place and title as professors of Care, Concern, Action, and Tough Love.

~Taking Back Our Communities~

Money alone injected into a poor or crime-ridden community is not going to change the conditions within that community. You've heard the saying that you can throw all the money at a problem and it never goes away; well, we've had local, state, and federal governments try to do just that for some of the inner-city communities with little to no results. You can give people sufficient money to pay off their bills or build them a new house and think that the problem is fixed, and within a couple of years they are right back where they started because you gave them the fish opposed to teaching them how to fish.

This scenario plays out almost every Thanksgiving or Christmas when churches or community groups provide meals to the needy. Although this is a noble and worthwhile cause, the results are usually the same: the person or family who received relief was right back in the same boat after the holiday period. Money is definitely part of the equation, but there are other aspects that must be taken into account to help these communities. Hope has to be restored to those living in the neighborhoods, access to examples of success have to be consistently present, educational opportunities must exist, and viable programs to assist the community must be present to make a significant difference.

I can't overemphasize the importance of education, because it is the ticket for the young to better their plight and hopefully give back by helping someone else. I personally know human relations are a key component to making changes within these communities, and this has been demonstrated in many experiments across the country.

§ In Savannah, Georgia, mentors were paired off with

young mothers to provide advice and counseling, and parents who were on the brink of losing their children were paired with experienced parents. As a result, the black infant mortality rate in the area decreased by almost 45 percent, foster care placements declined by 25 percent, and teen pregnancy dropped by some 12 percent.

§ In Oakland, California, social support systems similar to mentorship programs, aimed at keeping pregnant women healthy, resulted in a 50 percent decrease in the black infant mortality rate.

§ In Baltimore, Maryland, over a hundred outreach groups concentrated their efforts in one of the poorer neighborhoods to transform it into a thriving self-sufficient community. After a couple of years, the infant mortality and violent crime rate decreased approximately 20 percent, school attendance increased, and hundreds of residents found jobs.

Within these programs you had dedicated folks who regularly provided genuine advice that created trust, making the guidance more palatable than if it had come from someone who had never stepped foot in the neighborhood. For the recipients of these programs, hope was restored because they saw living evidence; they saw people who achieved all the things that they were advising on a daily or weekly basis. These processes are not a twice-a-year deal or a media event where some of the more blessed blacks rally to clean a park or read books to disadvantaged children or bring awareness to an issue through a walk-a-thon. Don't be fooled into thinking that these results come easily; they don't, because it takes hard work from blacks who are willing to give back to the community.

In conjunction with these initiatives, locally elected officials must be held accountable by the community to ensure that job programs for youth, reduced or affordable daycare services, and educational programs to certify skill laborers are available. One of the primary goals of community leaders and elected officials in poorer communities should be to ensure there are adequate and affordable daycare services. We all know that a single mother or even a couple with menial jobs can't make it without affordable daycare services. More importantly, you can't expect welfare (Temporary Assistance for Needy Families/TANF) recipients who have children to get off welfare or be successful if there are no provisions for their children while they are working or attending job training.

Equally important is meaningful employment for the youth within the community. If you took time to vote for your local leaders, then they ought to be active in the community and at city hall fighting for the resources necessary to make your community better.

When crime takes root and flourishes in our neighborhoods, we need to go into the garden and remove the weeds. Crime needs young children to grow and night to fertilize its roots. When we don't know where our kids are at night, crime is often on the prowl for a meal. When we have a rash of senseless killings, robberies, drive by shootings, and carjackings, it's not necessarily the time to run to the government; it's time to gather the folks in the community to take actions, to understand the problem, and formalize an action plan. What do you want the city council to do? Enact a law against drive by shootings? Or hold a ceremony declaring war on carjackings?

What is needed is a crime task force of the law-abiding citizens within the neighborhood to set attainable goals and objectives to reduce crime and make their neighborhood safer and less appealing for criminals. What are some of the things this task force can do?

(1) ensure proper lighting is available throughout the neighborhood; criminals and mischievous kids don't want to be seen;

(2) establish a rapport with the police; officials of the task force should engage the local police and let them know that they are welcomed and wanted in the neighborhood;

(3) ensure a representative attends all city council meetings and voices the concerns of the neighborhood; like the Minutemen, the community needs to be able to assemble in the council meetings when it's in their interest to demonstrate by numbers;

(4) identify abandon property and insist that the local government do something about it;

(5) host socials on a frequent basis where neighbors can get to know each other and voice their concerns;

(6) establish a clean-up day, maybe once a quarter or

twice a year, where the task force and neighbors clean their yards and public areas; an unkempt area is more appealing to a criminal; and

(7) establish a watch program to report suspicious behavior to the police.

~Trifling Brothers~

We have all heard that the black male is one of the next mammals to go into extinction. The black male is being made extinct by black on black crime, incarceration, and the epidemic proportions of brothers who are down low. Females on this planet outnumber males, reducing the chances of a female of finding a long-term mate. For black females, the issue of finding an eligible mate is further exacerbated by the number of black males that are off limits for one reason or another. The small population of black males from which a woman has to choose shrinks even further when you take into account the married brothers. What is left is a few good brothers who are looking for that special mate, and the leftover brothers who I consider trifling because they are not incarcerated at the moment or don't have a job and ain't looking for one or have no goals except for immediate gratification. The straight single brothers who have it going on are in a seller's market; they can demand the buyers (sistas) to bid on the highest price and pay the closing costs, and they can demand an escalation clause before closure (marriage or commitment).

Then you have the trifling brothers who are shallow shells parading around as if they are the bomb; they are a bomb, waiting to explode to cause destruction for anything in the immediate vicinity. Let me categorize the trifling brothers: these are the men in age but boys in maturity who think it's cool to depend on a sista to take care of their existence, these are the men in age but boys in maturity who totally shirk their parental responsibilities. Let me break it down further: they pay no child support nor do they devote any time raising their children. These are the men in age but boys in maturity who in their late thirties and forties still aspire to be the next Tu Pac. These are the men in age but boys in maturity who think that impregnating many women makes them more of a man.

I know this firsthand because I see and hear it all the time from my experiences during the many mentorship programs that I've headed. That gets me to another category of trifling brothers who think they are sperm depositors and relinquish all responsibility after they have deposited their manhood. These brothers usually don't pay any child support, leaving the woman to fend for herself financially, parentally, and emotionally. The U.S. Census Bureau reported in 2001 that 63 percent of black families are headed by a single parent; do the math, and you find that a large percentage of those families live in poverty and that compared with other races they have a higher percentage of delinquent young men and higher crime rates from these unguided young men.

The damage caused by these so-called fathers can be irreparable, especially for the male as he witnesses his mother struggling to make ends meet, sees the men come in and out of her life, and has no male figure in the house to emulate. These sons need and deserve a consistent positive male role model in their life whether it is a grandfather, uncle, older brother, or male friend.

Some people will say that there are many examples of women who raised their son without a consistent male figure in his life and the young man turned out to be a productive citizen. I agree, there have been thousands of success stories, but I can also point out five tragedies for every success story of a woman raising a male child by herself. If you don't believe me, go to the prisons, jails, and juvenile detention centers. I'm not advocating that a young black boy raised in a single-parent home will never turn out to be a productive citizen, but I am willing to say that the chances of success in life for a young black boy raised in a two-parent home (mother and father) increase exponentially.

During the Kappa League mentorship program, we would sometimes take the parents (mostly single mothers) aside so that they could discuss and share issues they encountered with their sons. In one of those discussions, I overheard a parent ask what she should or could do to raise her son to be a man. Another parent with an older son stated that "a woman can't raise a boy to be a man. It takes a man to raise a boy, but do the best you can and sometimes things will turn out all right." This is coming straight from a single parent who is educated and doing her best to support her family.

Then we have another category of trifling brothers who pay child support and think they have fulfilled their responsibilities by sending a check each month. Some of these brothers resent the fact that they have to pay, and continually complain that they were tricked or that the mother and child don't need that much money to survive. These brothers are not involved at all in the child's life and if asked to attend a PTA meeting, sporting event, or parent-teacher conference, they quickly inform the mother that they have done their part by sending money each month. These brothers don't understand why their child rebukes them when he or she becomes an adult; they try to rationalize with the child that it was better for them to stay away to keep peace with the mother or that they met their parental obligation by sending a monthly check. Some of these brothers will have the audacity to ask their child to help them once they get up in age; I know, because my biological grandfather begged my mother to take care of him when his days of fancy footing and cruising the streets had left his body into a shell of a man.

Next, we have the player players who stumble and bumble through life as if they were carefree birds flying from nest to nest for shelter and food. These trifling brothers have huge dreams, but the only dream they have realized lately has been a wet one. These brothers prey on our sistas and to my amazement become pretty successful at manipulating a sista to sponsor them for a rent-free place to stay, two to three meals a day, gas for their car, and an allowance.

Finally, you have the down-low brothers who are both trifling and dangerous. These brothers disguise themselves as family men, business leaders, politicians, bankers, lawyers, and professional sports athletes. You won't see them parading around like drag queens. Many of them have beautiful girlfriends or wives, but there is a darker side of them that only other down-low brothers know how to identify. These brothers begin by experimenting and, like crack, get addicted to that dark side of life where they are Jekyll or Hyde depending on when and where they are. When I first read about this, I couldn't believe that of all people, a select group of brothers would consider a lifestyle that could hurt so many people. I have more respect for the straight-up gay man or woman who doesn't try to trick folks. Why in the world would a black man want to be "down low" when he could choose from the very lightest sista to the caramel complexioned sista to the blackest big-hipped sista and oh, by the way, these sistas have good jobs and many are very successful in their careers. I get hives thinking about two black men with crusty feet and ashy legs lying up next to each other. Get a grip, "down low" brothers; you're causing more harm than good to the heterosexuals. Be one way or the other, choose a side, and stick to it.

Looking at the various trifling brothers, one can understand why sistas are so bitter and skeptical when it comes to choosing a companion; however, brothers as a whole are not totally to blame for the situation. I think we can also place some of the blame on the women of the '90s movement that told a woman that she was empowered to do everything that a man could do and that in reality she didn't need a man. I'm all for and about a sophisticated, educated, business-driven black woman. I'm all for a woman getting paid the same rate as a man and being respected for what she can contribute to the business or corporation. However, I'm not down for the sistas who think they don't need a man in their life to raise a family or to grow old together. The '90s women movement planted such a seed in some women, which had devastating affects, especially for black women.

Single straight brothers, if you are reading this portion, then I can tell you where to find your soul mate: CHURCH. She just prayed for you and is sitting on the ninth pew waiting on you to claim her.

~Somewhat Trifling Sistas~

I want my daughter to become a strong, independent, educated and a self-respecting woman. I also want her to have a loving husband and family. I'm sure fathers and mothers twenty and twenty-five years my senior wanted the same for their daughters, and I'm certain that they wanted things to fall in place in a particular order.

I stress the importance of education and independence to my daughter, and she understands. I've told her to ensure that she has her own stuff (car, house, money, etc.) and never place herself in a situation where she has to totally rely on a man or to support one. I also told her that she has to be active in the community and has to stay abreast of current events.

My wife and I verbally established her life's path, which does not include a serious relationship until her education is complete and career established. By dictating these milestones to her, am I setting her up to be a somewhat trifling sista? After discussing this with some of my male friends, I have come to the conclusion that I am indeed setting her up to become a somewhat trifling sista. What I have not told her is to have balance in her life when she gets older and that means it's OK to develop a mutual relationship with a young man without sacrificing her dignity, honor, and her life goals.

The '90s movement told a woman that she didn't need a man and certainly not until she saved the world from world hunger or became the next Bill Gates. As a result, a lot of well-intentioned young women focused all of their energy on career, community or church-related causes. Many of these women had a plan etched in concrete on when, how, and the date that they would establish the family with two children and a dog, and it wasn't until most of their career goals had been reached; what they didn't understand is that love and compatibility don't work on a person's timetable.

While they were being all they could be, these women were missing golden opportunities to establish relationships with young men who may have had the same interests and same goals and who would support them in their cause to make a difference or a name for themselves. Instead, some, maybe a lot, chose brief relationships where no one would get hurt (maintenance man) or interfere with their goals. Simultaneously, the pool of educated and eligible black men began to shrink in their area to the point that the few eligible, educated, and straight men became known commodities in their single's world.

Now, when that career-driven young lady is still single in her late thirties or early forties after reaching many of her milestones, she realizes that she has to act quickly to get the husband and family. What she doesn't know is that the independence and drive she once depended upon can become a liability if not carefully considered. Over the years, she has become set in her ways and is unwilling to let the man take the lead. If she does allow him to take the lead, then she second-guesses his every move simply because she has effectively led men in the boardroom, church room and during rallies.

She now reflects back on the maintenance men that she used to satisfy her sexual desires and thinks that if she used them, others will do the same to her; she now thinks that every man wants to sleep with her and does not want to get to know her. She becomes critical and cynical of men because the pool has shrunk so much that she is running into the jive broke players with bad credit and little to no education. The few eligible, educated, and straight men don't have a chance, because her past experiences have taken control, and they tell her that something is wrong with a man if he is still available. If she dates the successful black man then she puts him through a grueling test that she has contrived to test his worthiness and you know the result: nine times out of ten, he fails. He fails because she is unwilling to compromise and he fails because it just ain't worth it no matter, how hard he tries. Sadly, they both fail a test that could have been aced if they worked as a team, trusting and respecting each other.

This is a scary scenario, so, I will continue to emphasize the importance of education and career to my daughter, but will also inform her that she has to have balance in her life. I will tell her that when she gets that high-paying job or becomes a leader over many men and women, to leave the drive, aggressiveness, and all of the manly traits that make her a success at the job and connect with that feminine side when she is with her male companion. I'm sure he will appreciate her accomplishments and will want to know about her career, but at the same time, he wants to know that he is expected and trusted to take the lead in their relationship. If she maintains balance, she can find the soul mate who is willing to support her educational and career goals while at the same time establishing a family.

Single woman, I know you just prayed for your man, and God has answered your prayer. He is the one who has been speaking to you for the last few Sundays and is walking down the aisle to give his tithes, but you paid him no attention because he is not the Denzel you were looking for, nor does he have the appeal of a Michael Jordan. He drives a truck to church, he owns a painting business, and he makes decent money, but does not have the status you want to brag to your girlfriends about. Nevertheless, he is a good, hard-working man and will devote his every moment to you and your family... that is, if you give him a chance.

Chapter VI

Black Monday, Black Massacre, Black Day

"We have become ninety-nine percent money mad. The method of living at home modestly and within our income, laying by systematically for the proverbial rainy day which is due to come, can almost be listed among the lost arts." George Washington Carver

~The Real Lay-away Plan~

THE TITLE of this chapter includes just some of the names that are given to historic tragedies in American History, whether it be the stock market crash in 1987 (Black Monday) or the atrocities in Tulsa, Oklahoma, in 1921 (Black Massacre) or 9/11 (Black Day), there probably stands a good chance that the word black will precede the event or day to highlight just how bad it was.

I think the only thing that refers to black in a positive light is an economical state of being in which there is positive cash flow. In this regard, blacks have seen and endured many black Mondays, massacres and days, but too few of us have realized the economical state of being in the black.

Here is my testimony on being in the black; however, I'm just a couple of paychecks from being in the red. As I mentioned earlier, Gary helped me out tremendously by reintroducing mutual funds and other saving vehicles to me and, more importantly, a strategy to take what I had and increase it two or threefold. This strategy wasn't some miraculous formula and would not produce immediate earnings; it was designed to produce over the long term. It involved no scratch on/off lottery tickets, pyramid schemes, investing in your son or daughter to make them a professional athlete or rapper, bets on fights or games, or befriending an elderly or sick relative to receive an inheritance. *(A survey published by Minority Wealth magazine found that minorities had a higher confidence in building wealth by taking their chances on the lottery than in the traditional methods of saving and investing into practical methods such as retirement or mutual funds. What's sad is that 60 percent of the minorities surveyed stated that they understood the lottery better than the traditional methods of wealth building, and that lottery information was more readily available.)* There were a few simple things you had to do to develop a comfortable life for yourself and family. I must put in a disclaimer that this strategy won't work unless you have a job with a steady income; you don't have to make six figures for this to work either.

Are you ready? First, thank God for what he has given

you in the form of talent and resources, then look around at your possessions and at yourself and be honestly thankful. This spiritual moment will help you realize the blessings that you've already received, and then you will begin to picture some of the folks who are or were worse off than you. It will also ground you as to what is important. As I said earlier, everyone is not destined to have the million-dollar house with swimming pool, tennis courts, and luxury cars to fill the three-car garage. Another spiritual moment that will place you in the right frame of mind is to give to your favorite charity or church on a consistent basis. I think the proverb of "it's better to give than to receive" is fitting to place you in the mind-set of being benevolent, giving, and caring and de-emphasizes the materialistic craving that so many of us possess.

If you haven't done so already, make a commitment to take care of what you have. If you own a house and car, then ensure that the yard and outside and inside of the house stay in pristine condition. I say this because it will gauge you when you consider upgrading. If you are unable to take care of what you have, then it will be even more difficult to take care of something that is larger or more expensive. Therefore, you should seriously take into consideration the maintenance fees for the car that you may want to purchase or the time and money you will have to invest into the upkeep of the yard and house. So many people only take into the account the mortgage payments or car payments, and when they land in their dream car or dream house they soon realize they don't have the resources (money and time) to keep up their car or house and, believe me, it shows.

Secondly, get an assessment of what other people think about you. Get a report from the three major credit bureaus as well as your credit score. Your credit report is your reputation, and it says a lot about you as an individual. This is your resume, and people who can influence others to get you in that house or car will want to know if you honor your word. I didn't understand the importance of paying my bills on time until I wanted to purchase my second car and couldn't because of my credit, even though I could easily afford it. Since that time, I have been very conscientious about paying my bills on time and ensuring that my credit report reflected the type of person I wanted others to be impressed by. Maxed-out credit cards, consecutive months late of car payments, and just plain late payments on small bills didn't help the situation. They tell you to get your credit report every six months; I've tried to do just that since I've found discrepancies in my credit report and was able to rectify them. Also, pulling my credit report on a frequent basis was like taking an appetite suppressant as I noticed my bills dwindling and number of revolving accounts reduced.

I really didn't understand the power of the credit report and ratings until I purchased a second house. By this time, the credit baggage I had been dragging along was now gone and my ratings had improved to the point that creative financing and low interest rates were available. It was an eureka moment, an awakening, a rebirth all in one when I realized how the other side was able to afford the houses, cars, boats etc. These folks didn't necessarily make six-digit salaries; many of them made decent money, lived within their means, had great credit, and saved or invested a portion of their earnings on a consistent basis. When it came time to purchase their dream house, they were offered many financing options opposed to the two options for those with bad credit (1) come back when you have enough for a down payment and are able to demonstrate that you can pay your bills on time or (2) 10 percent down payment, 4 points higher than the norm on a fixed-rate mortgage.

Third, once you've made peace, conducted an assessment of your bills, and established a date to pay the excess bills, then keep a credit card but look at closing out the cards and revolving accounts. Bottom line, develop a plan to pay off most of your credit cards and start using cash to pay for those wants and needs. If your creditor offers a draft payment option, then by all means have your payments come directly from your checking account. Your mortgage and car note at a minimum should come directly from your saving or checking account. If you have the major bills automatically coming from your checking or saving account, then you're assured your payments will be on time and you won't be tempted to send in a late payment because you saw an outfit or concert ticket that was not in your budget.

More importantly, conduct a financial review for the family. The adults of the household should periodically review the credit reports, monthly bills, and the financial strategy. If children are in the household, then they should be educated at an early age about financial responsibility. We live in a very materialistic society and if we don't start educating our young at an early age, then we will continue to be the largest group of consumers and the smallest group who own something that appreciates. I regularly tell my children about the stupid mismanagement of my money when I first started out, and I also tell them how I overcame the debt by taking an appetite suppressant and living within my means.

Fourth, if you're considering upgrading or expanding your portfolio, establish a range with which you will be financially comfortable. Don't be pressured no matter what that salesman or real estate agent tells you can afford; you have to pay the bills, not them. I've heard people say buy up; that might work for some, but I can tell you it doesn't work for most. Buying up sometimes means that you could be treading water, and all it takes to sink you under is a splash created by a goldfish.

One of the hardest things to do is to resist the impulse ego purchase. Your real estate agent or salesman will pump you up so that you think you are Bill Gates and then the ego kicks in and next thing you're saying is "I can do this." But if you're not careful, you'll find yourself in a fish bowl, fearing the splash of the goldfish. Believe me, I've made my share of impulse ego buying and I was fearing that goldfish as well. Once you've made your purchase, remember the newness will wear off, so be prepared for the commitment. Again, be thankful, enjoy your possession and maintain it.

I can almost guarantee you that after you've ridden on Cloud Nine for a while; the Joneses will pay your family a visit. The Joneses aren't your neighbors who purchased a smoother, sexier car than you, nor are they the relatives who were just admiring your house a couple of months ago and recently purchased a house that dwarfs yours in comparison and style, nor are they the ones who just complimented you about your diamond ring or outfit and now they have the diamond that is so large that you need to exercise your finger to hold it upright. Nope, the Joneses are the spoiled mini-me who sits on your shoulder and always finds something wrong with what you have, or is always telling you that you are better and the others shouldn't have something better than you. Trust me, the Joneses will come when you least expect them, but you must take a deep breath and tell yourself over and over that you are happy with what you have and that you made the right decision for you. Thank the man above and release those materialistic cravings. Remember to be thankful and know that material things do not make the person... success comes in many forms.

~I Want You to Have the Things I Never Had~

Have you ever met any parents that didn't want the best for their child or children? Remember when you were growing up and you said to yourself that you wanted to do a little better than your parents? I don't care what socioeconomic level you study, you will always find a large percentage of parents who will do almost anything to ensure their children have the latest and most fashionable clothes, game, toy, computer gadget, or fees to participate in an extracurricular activity. If the parents don't have the funds, then they will scrape, borrow, and beg to get whatever funds are needed. It doesn't matter to the parents that it may not be within their budget, because they have rationalized that their child will not go through childhood wanting or missing out.

Instead of saying no, "I can't afford it now," some parents will even miss paying a bill so that their child can have what they desire. This phenomenon transcends race. If you go in a poor black neighborhood and look at the children, you will find that some of them have the latest and most expensive sneakers, computer gadgets, or whatever is fashionable.

One of the young men that I mentor lives in Southeast D.C., a rough and tough environment. When I picked him up one Saturday, we had a conversation about clothing, and he informed me that there were many kids at his school who had the latest, most expensive sneakers that cost as much as $175.00. Why would a parent who has difficult making ends meet spend that much on a child? What's wrong with saying, "I can't afford that type of sneaker but will get you some that are within my means but are nice and fashionable"? My mother teaches at a predominately black middle school where many of the kids come from poor families, and she will be the first to tell you that many of the kids come to school with the latest and best outfits the clothing stores have to offer. However, when it is time to buy something related to their education, they don't have the money.

In many cases, regardless of economic status, we as parents buy items carte blanche, even if the child has not performed well in school or has misbehaved at home or really doesn't need them. In the grand scheme of things, it's the parents' responsibility to provide the necessary environment and tools for a child to be successful. I don't think the most expensive items will help any child accomplish that goal. This is especially troubling in the black communities, where we as a people are proportionately the largest consumers in America yet we trail behind most in appreciable property ownership. In our efforts to compensate for the things that we did not have or to ensure our children don't go without or to show our love through materialistic things, we have created generations of young men and women who don't value the hard work that goes behind getting those things. Don't get me wrong. I believe that we should do our best for our kids, but the "wants" should not be handed out on a silver platter. Many of us have left the one key component that sometimes separates the child who will go on in life to be successful from the one who will stumble through life—a work ethic.

A work ethic comes in many forms but here are a few

that come to my mind: works diligently in school to do the very best, does chores around the house to a standard without constant reminding, has a part-time job, or does odd jobs to obtain what he or she wants. My parents and many of my friends' parents established a work ethic in us at a very early age. If you wanted, not needed, something, then you became an entrepreneur (mowing grass/cleaning houses/babysitting) or got a job at the local chain store or did odd jobs with the local handyman. Grades and good behavior were not factors in getting what you desired because those were the givens… you were expected to do those things. As I grew older, I realized that it was up to me to get the things that I wanted; my parents provided everything for me to be successful, but they weren't going to get the luxuries. So, when I was old enough to work, I got a job at Golden Corral washing dishes to get the more expensive clothes that I wanted. Instead of a new car after graduation, I received my dead uncle's fifteen-year-old car and in their eyes, it got me from point A to B; if I wanted something better then I had to earn it myself, and I did.

People always joke about the Asians or Jamaicans who come to America and work two, three, four, or five jobs to make a living and yet you rarely see them in or with the most expensive anything. They live within their means and instill a work ethic in their children at a very early age. Now here is how I see the possible repercussions of giving a child without a work ethic everything he or she wants. (*Disclaimer: There are successful folks who were spoiled rotten but understood the power of hard work.*) You probably even know these folks who are in their late thirties, forties, or even fifties who bounce from one job to another, bounce back and forth staying at their place and their parents' home, and are always borrowing money from folks to get things they really don't need. These folks were provided everything to be successful and more but were not taught a work ethic, so they became adults who are still dependent on someone, and it's usually the living parents. These folks come from all different economic and educational backgrounds. The ones who come from a middle-income family with college-educated parents more than likely dropped out of college after the first year or so. They are always living above their means because they don't know how or don't have the patience to work and save to get the things they want. All that registers in their minds is that their parents effortlessly purchased the nice house they lived in, bought new cars every two or three years, took them on vacations, and gave them what they wanted regardless of the situation. They never saw, were taught, or experienced the work, the planning, the saving, and the sacrificing that the parents endured to get them those nice things. These folks often become obsessed with obtaining material things either for themselves or for their children to show that they are a success. Their parents never get a chance to enjoy their retirement because they are either supporting them or their grandchildren.

While the parents are living, these adult children become leeches that drain the parents' retirement pay, savings, and any type of pension plan they have. Instead of scrapping and saving to get the things they want, sometimes unintentionally, they hover overhead like vultures waiting for the parent or parents to die so that they can receive the insurance payouts, house, or whatever they think should be bequeathed to them. Believe it or not, that is Plan A to getting the bank account, house, or car. The siblings who are doing well go through hell as they see their parents' retirement plans drained and comfort of living diminished in front of their eyes.

After the parents die, it becomes a life-changing event for the successful children who assisted the parents with their mortgage or paid a couple of bills or watched over them during their illness. Many of the successful siblings are in disbelief as they see their own flesh and blood fight and argue with them over who should get what. The funeral arrangements are usually coordinated by the successful children while the other children sit around waiting for the funeral and meeting with the lawyer.

This scenario may be the extreme, but I'm sure you've witnessed something like this. If you don't teach a child a work ethic, then he or she will have a much harder time trying to build a comfortable living for themselves.

Chapter VII

Politically Correct or Correct-less

"Politics, it seems to me, for years, or all too long, has been concerned with right or left instead of right or wrong." *Richard Armour*

~Democrats vs. Republicans~

THE MAJORITY of blacks tend to be in the Democratic Party. Why is that? Is there something wrong with a brother or sister changing parties? What are the principles of each party? Do we associate with a party because our parents associated with that party or because the people in a party are more like us? I guarantee you that over half of the voting population has no clue of the principles or tenets of their party, and probably many of them aren't even aware of their candidate's stance on issues.

Before we talk about specific issues, let's get a common operating picture of the two major parties and what they stand for. The Republican Party was Abraham Lincoln's party and is the party that emancipated slaves. After the Civil War ended in 1865, you had the Reconstruction period during which Northern soldiers occupied the South and ensured the safety of blacks. This period lasted about a decade and during this time, blacks prospered somewhat in the South. There were black U.S. representatives, senators, local government leaders, and even a black governor. A dark movement in the Democratic Party emerged to reverse the gains of blacks; this movement reared its ugly head in the form of the Klan and Jim Crow in the early 1900s after the withdrawal of Northern troops and officials from the South. Later on, a group called the Dixiecrats ruled the South with their hate-filled principles and ideologies. Blacks still belonged to the Republican Party through the sixties, and in the late sixties and early seventies a flip flop occurred in which blacks shifted to the Democratic Party and very conservative whites moved to the Republican Party.

Today, you have those who consider themselves conservative, meaning less government, low taxes, fiscal responsibility, pro-military, and anti-abortion, and then you have a group who considers themselves more compassionate to the plight of those less fortunate, environmental friendly, pro-abortion, group responsibility, pro-military but not at the expense of social solutions. As I look at both parties, I see sound principles in each; if you had a menu option to choose, you could get a party more representative of the American population.

You see, you have a few of the extremes of each party

who force their ideology on the majority of a group; they somehow get a platform or have the means to voice their opinion and before you know it, they are setting the agenda for the rest of the party. Even though the majority may not agree with them they are too afraid to tell the few extremists to shut up, sit down, and color. They don't want to be seen as having strife within their own party... they call this inclusiveness. How do you think the Iraq war started or the gay marriage movement? It surely wasn't the majority; both were started by a few in each party who felt so passionate and convicted about their views that they got the ball rolling. Both issues have or will snowball us till the majority are trampled into submission.

Here is my summary of some of the major principles and tenets of both parties:

§ **Democrats on foreign policy**... Strong international alliances are the cornerstone of foreign policy. The threat from international terrorism and rogue states requires a new era of alliances led by the United States, based on mutual respect and shared vision. **Republicans on foreign policy**... Nations that support terrorism are just as guilty. Pursue a comprehensive strategy against weapons of mass destruction on proliferation. Provide new strategies to help poor nations and objectives of assistance and the strategies must change.

§ **Democrats on the economy**... The most effective means of increasing opportunity for families is a high-quality, good-paying job. Commit to expanding economic opportunity to all Americans and creating the new jobs of the future. **Republicans on the economy**... Cut taxes to stimulate the economy and encourage re-investment. Be fiscally responsible and reduce government spending. Support free trade that is fair.

§ **Democrats on education**... Meet the nation's responsibilities by ensuring that our schools have the resources they need to help our kids meet high standards. Expand educational opportunities for college by providing relief from skyrocketing college tuition; increase the size and access to Pell grants and support proven programs that encourage more young people to attend and succeed in college. **Republicans on education**... Promote school choice and home-schooling. Support voluntary student-initiated prayer in school.

§ **Democrats on civil rights and justice**... Unwavering support of equal opportunity for all Americans. Passage of the Civil Rights Act and the Voting Rights Act are key as well as ensuring reauthorization of the Voting Rights Act in 2007. Vigorously support expanding opportunities in jobs, health care benefits, and education and enforcement of civil rights laws. States should determine marriage criteria, no change to the Constitution defining marriage. **Republicans on civil rights and justice**... Affirmative access, without preferences or set-asides. States should not recognize gay marriage from other states. Support of the Patriot Act because it is used to track terrorist activity. Support the advancement of women in the military however homosexuality is incompatible with military service.

§ **Democrats on abortion**... .Pro-choice; a woman should have the right to determine her fate. **Republicans on abortion**... .Promote adoption and abstinence and add a Human Life Amendment to Constitution.

§ **Democrats on gun control**... Certain restrictions such as child safety locks, waiting period, background checks and banning of designated assault rifles are necessary to protect citizens and track criminals. **Republicans on gun control**... Open more public land for hunting, no frivolous gun lawsuits and no gun licensing.

On some of these issues you will notice significant differences; on others, the positions reflect the standard line voters want to hear. No matter where you live in this great country of ours, I guarantee you that there has been an issue in your local area or a stance that an elected official has taken that has impacted you in some form or fashion.

~If You Can See, Why Cast a Blind Vote? ~

I used to do the thing that most people do when it comes time to choose a candidate; "Oh, they are black or oh, they are white, so I'll vote for them" or "Oh, they are Democrat or Republican so I'll vote for them." Not anymore.

Here is why I'm so passionate with politics and so opinionated in my views. The experience that drove me to say enough is enough came when my county's school district almost lost its accreditation because some renegade members of the school board decided to fire the superintendent without due cause. I didn't have a problem with them firing the superintendent, but it was the way they went about it and how they handled the public relations afterward that ticked me off and caused such an uproar among parents and concerned citizens. There was a power shift in my school board after we elected a new chair and more black members.

Before I moved to the county, I was told that the black superintendent was fired, let go, or whatever you want to call it for no reason. Oh, by the way, we still paid his salary even when we hired a new superintendent. The new superintendent had been on board almost two years and after the power shift, the new board members decided to play tit for tat and fired the superintendent when he showed up at a school board meeting. I believe both men were competent and were good for the county; however, they both paid for the demographic change from a mostly white county to a mostly black county.

The way the second man was fired was almost comical and drew so much attention throughout Atlanta. The board chair and her followers decided to have a little special vote without knowing the rules on how it was supposed to be done. The board of regents took notice and began an investigation into the matter. Meanwhile, the superintendent prepared a lawsuit, the board chair and board members who voted to oust him couldn't explain why they fired him, the newspapers were having a field day with this issue, and parents were putting for sale signs in their yards. The board was directed to conduct a national search and they did what they thought was a national search by handpicking a black administrator in Atlanta. I didn't have a problem with them picking a black administrator, but I didn't think they conducted a national search as directed by the board of regents, nor did the county residents or the board of regents.

Over the next couple of months the regents put their foot down and mandated another national search, saying that otherwise, all schools in the county would lose their accreditation. More for sale signs went up, and it was primarily the middle- and higher-income families with school-aged children who were getting the heck out of the county.

So what happens when this group of folks flees an area? (1) No meaningful industry will move to an area or county that has a suspect school district... one of the first things a large business will ask the county officials or research is about the schools. Sure, the county will continue to have the barber shops, beauty salons, manicure salons, and fast-food joints locate in the area, but don't expect to have corporate headquarters or white-collar jobs moving to an area that has school problems. (2) Property values stagnate or even decrease because you now have a smaller pool of folks to purchase homes. (3) Developers won't even think about building more executive housing in the area now because your middle- and higher-income folks have fled the area; thus, more so-called "affordable housing" and more apartments are built. To have a thriving and viable city or county, you need a mixture of all income groups.

I wanted answers; therefore, I wrote an e-mail and letter to my school board representatives (one black and the other white) requesting an explanation about why they ousted the superintendent and what they were doing to conduct another national search. The white school board member e-mailed me back and stated that she was against the coup and voted accordingly. She assured me she would obey the mandates of the board of regents. I never heard from the black representative for whom I had just voted months earlier. Because the school board was a predominately black school board and all except one of the black board members had voted the white superintendent out, the racial overtones took root. Soon, the folks in the community, business leaders, and media began to draw lines. A series of community meetings were scheduled to help folks understand what happened and how the community could get involved to fix it. We were now paying two superintendents, but didn't have one to occupy an office.

I attended one of the first meetings sponsored by the local NAACP chapter and local churches. The media were there to capture sound bites for the nightly news and reporters there to write columns. Although the meeting was held at a black church, I was pleased to see a large representation of white citizens. The meeting started off with a brief summary of events and then the floor was opened for folks to vent their concerns. I had no intention of speaking because many of the parents voiced my concerns and asked the questions I would have asked concerning the national search and impact on the county. However, when most of the black school board members entered the church and sat directly behind me, my blood began to boil. It began to boil for several reasons (1) I voted for one of the members without doing any research and this vote had come back to haunt me as well as many other parents and citizens. (2) In my opinion, some of the new members were in over their heads holding these positions of authority; it had absolutely nothing to do with race, but with management experience and competence. (3) You could never get a straight answer on why he was fired and what they were doing to make good on the national search. (4) The board members had a chip on their shoulder as if two wrongs make a right. (5) It appeared every civil rights person in the area was solicited to scream racial discrimination.

I couldn't hold my seat any longer after the Muslim from Temple # whatever in downtown Atlanta talked about how this was a racial issue and that we should support our sisters. He went on to state that we should trust them to make the right decisions and support whatever decision they make. He also said that white folks had done it to us, so we should do the same to them. To me, it was as if someone had invaded my home and was telling me how to run my household. Most folks in that meeting, black and white, wanted two things: (1) an explanation of why the superintendent was fired and (2) when would the board authorize a national search. Up to this point, the board leadership refused to conduct another national search, and the clock was ticking on the districts accreditation.

After the Muslim sat down, I jumped up, went to the front, and confronted him about his true intentions of getting air time and sparking racial divisiveness. I told him that since he didn't reside in the county, he shouldn't try to speak for the citizens. I then turned and focused on the school board members and told my representative that I e-mailed her and wrote her a letter and that she didn't have the decency to address my concerns. Before I sat down, I implored the citizens to rally together so that our collective voices could be heard by the board of regents.

This meeting along with a few more meetings put tremendous pressure on the board, and at the next meeting there was a record crowd gathered to speak and force the board to authorize a national search. The scene seemed like an execution watch. The school board room was an old renovated auditorium or court room with a balcony. It was painted in white and folding chairs made up two sections of the room. The board members sat on an elevated platform with microphones positioned in front of them, so the anxious crowd could hear their comments. Every seat, every corner, every aisle was full of blacks and whites evenly spread throughout the room. Folks in the balcony leaned over the ledge to hear every word that was said. News media were everywhere, waiting to interview parents, students, and citizens as they departed the room.

Civil rights leaders were positioned up front; sheriff deputies and police were strategically located throughout the room prepared for a riot.

Students, parents, and citizens were allotted time to voice their concerns to the school board. There were many calls from blacks and whites for the immediate resignation of all members. The tension in the room was so thick that you could see it and feel it. The meeting finally started and shortly thereafter, an uproar from the crowd erupted when they heard the agenda. It didn't contain the national search as mandated by the board of regents.

The police and sheriff deputies moved quickly to protect the board members, because some of the folks began to shout obscenities and a few took steps toward the platform before being restrained. That eruption put things in perspective for the chairperson and her followers; people were dead serious about this and they weren't going to allow these women to screw up their lives. The chairperson added the topic after she received instructions from the regents or education representative on how to amend the agenda.

The topic was finally added and when it came time to deliberate and vote, these board members stated they opposed putting it on the agenda because they wanted to wait until their retreat to make a decision on whether and when to conduct another search. The chair put the motion to conduct a national search to a vote. The chair and her three followers abstained, but a victory was won when the remainder of the board voted to conduct a national search.

The chair and her followers were escorted out by the police to ensure their protection and life went on in my county. The search was conducted and we hired a black superintendent who is doing quite well. This incident severely hurt my county, not just the school system; it hurt any chances of a corporate headquarters relocating to the county.

The county is still recovering, but one lesson was learned from this incident: you don't blindly vote for a person, and you certainly don't vote for them simply because they are the same skin color. What could have been done to avoid scenarios like this one? Local leaders could have hosted a debate or an opportunity to get to know the candidates and maybe we would have been able to determine if that is the person we wanted to represent our county. Some counties host a debate for heavily contested races, which is worthwhile when trying to discern who has the skill sets and desire to do their best for the people. As noted by my testimony, politics has a direct impact on our lives; it has an even greater impact on the middle income and lower income levels. Think about it... political decisions to change abortion laws, crime laws such as three strikes and out, mandatory sentences for certain offenses, and so on.

If you're fortunate enough to be rich, then political decisions don't affect you unless its tax related such as the estate tax. The rich have the means to circumvent many of the political decisions, because money means access and power. I would like to focus on the changing political landscape to hone in on the matters of our time. Who suffers the most when extremists in each party push these issues to the national level? The minority.

I would like to focus on a couple of issues from both parties that have affected blacks. Again, I want to put in a disclaimer that this is my humble opinion. I 'm going to hit some topics that may, as the preacher says, "step on some feet"; therefore, put your boots on to absorb the weight of my foot.

~Foreign Policy Is Exactly That for Us Lately… It's Foreign~

More than ever before in our lives, we really have to consider how our foreign policy affects our lives. September 11 2001, brought this nation to a reality: no more are the vast oceans and land masses in the world a hedge or fortress of protection. Nowadays, you can instantly call someone half the way around the world or teleconference a person or group of people from opposite points on the earth. We can zap an e-mail in seconds to anywhere in the world, and flying from one hemisphere to another is almost akin to taking a bus from one town to another town within a state.

Technology has brought us that much closer together and now that we have that closeness, we need to learn how to be better neighbors. In the past, we entrusted those folks who were educated in political science or those who took the time to study a particular country to be our trusted agents and set our foreign policy agenda. That was OK before CNN, e-mail, video teleconference, blogs, and inexpensive flights to anywhere in the world. It was OK because we knew exactly who our enemy was and had the time to collect volumes of material on their habits, traditions, and culture.

Since the world has changed significantly after the Soviet Union's collapse, we need to take inventory on the possible changes, currents, and trends within our neighborhood. We've used the same approaches for collecting data that were prevalent when we knew our adversaries; these techniques and processes are now antiquated in the fluid and changing political environment.

Our recent foreign policy efforts have been as those of a kid who has just moved into a new neighborhood. Instead of trying to learn about the other kids, their quirks, their background, their playing habits, their hot buttons, and their loyalty levels, we've been the kid who stands afar and immediately draws conclusions based solely on what he sees. In my neighborhood and many others, you will find that you have a diverse group of people. These families have different cultures, traditions, values, religious beliefs, and viewpoints on life.

We had at least one family that was more affluent than the other neighbors; you could tell by the way they kept the yard, the types of cars in the driveway, the upgrades that were made to the house, and the type of toys their kids played with. These families were arrogant and most people didn't want to be around them. If they offered something to the other neighbors, then you could bet that there was a hidden agenda and you would end up paying dearly if you accepted. The children of these families were too good to play with the other kids, and when they did play with the other kids they were constantly criticizing the other kid's house, yard, or cars. These kids even had the audacity to tell you how you should live your life and how the way they lived was so much better than yours... they would say stuff such as "You do what on Sunday? That's stupid"; "You have to wait until your parents save up the money to get it?"

Then you had the families who moved into the neighborhood and just didn't understand how to be good neighbors. These were the families who didn't keep their yards up or who drove down the value of the other homes with their broken-down cars in the front yard and loud music at night. These were the hell raisers, and their kids usually were the bullies of the neighborhood. There were only a few folks in the neighborhood who they respected, and it sure wasn't the arrogant families.

Then you had the status quo or transparent neighbors, who did what was required to coexist in the neighborhood. These families comprised the majority of the neighborhood and did their part by maintaining their homes and respecting others within the neighborhood. These families also had their quirks, but once you understood them and they you, then there were no problems. You know the quirks I'm talking about... the ultra-religious family whose kids can't come outside to play on Sunday, or the family who has nine kids living in a three-bedroom house and no one outside of the family has been in the house to see how they accommodate all those people, or the family with the alcoholic father and everyone in the neighborhood knows that he hides his liquor in the shrubbery next to the vacant house.

Then you have the peacemakers, families who did well for themselves; everyone wanted to be around them. They maintained their house and their kids were the most popular kids around. These folks were compassionate yet strong, giving but not gullible, and open minded not closed. They were genuinely concerned about the folks in the neighborhood. All the other families knew if there was a problem that they couldn't resolve, they could count on the peacemakers to offer the right advice or adjudicate the issue. More importantly, everyone respected them and held them in high regard.

Which family is the United States? Not too long ago, I think we were viewed within the world community as the peacemakers of the world. However, our arrogance and neglect of getting to know our neighbors has made us that arrogant family that no one really respects. I don't attribute all of this to our current administration; this occurred over several administrations. However, hatred of Americans has never been so great.

To reverse this trend, I propose that we do a full court public relations campaign starting in the Middle East that emphasizes our values and the good things that we do around the world. As the minister states, you don't have to worry about the bad things getting broadcasted, but if you expect folks to know the good things about you, then someone is going to have to broadcast it.

Additionally, we should put aside our current approach of spreading democracy and concentrate on human rights within the countries to which we want to spread democracy. We should assist these countries in building institutions that can host a democratic society; you need a justice system, established and enforceable laws, infrastructure to support basic needs, and a body to ensure there are checks and balances within the government, just to name a few.

The ultraconservative wing of the Republican Party has this notion that you can establish a democracy by having a vote to elect a leader and government. Yes, if afforded the right to vote, people will vote, but this does not mean that you will have a democracy. It means that you have a popular leader and popular government; that does not equal a democracy. Until a country has met the basic needs of its citizens, values the civil liberties of all its citizens through enforcement of its laws, has the institutions and infrastructure critical to be self-dependent, and the will of the people then you won't be able to supplant democracy into a country. Remember, America called itself a democracy before the civil rights era, and during this time we still had a group of citizens who couldn't vote and didn't have the civil liberties afforded to the majority. Even though America had been in existence for some two hundred years and called it self a democracy, it wasn't a true form of democracy until the civil liberties of all citizens was available.

What happened to our foreign policy and planning after the invasion of Iraq? I'm not a Monday morning quarterback nor am I a person who says I told you so, but how in the world could we be so far off in our planning and intelligence of Iraq? By now, you should know that I was never in favor of the Iraq invasion. I felt we had Saddam contained and weakened through sanctions. I know he had weapons of mass destruction, but not the nuclear ones that we were really after. He had prevented inspectors into his country because the notion that he might actually have WMD kept him in power, kept his enemy Iran on its side of the border, and kept his nemesis Israel guessing. What if I was wrong and he did have nuclear weapons? I truly believe he was too afraid of losing power to use them or sell them to a terrorist. Saddam knew a strike initiated by him or a terrorist who was supplied a weapon by him meant total annihilation to his country, therefore no legacy.

Don't you think taking him down was a good thing? Absolutely, but if we are the policemen of the world, then we need to head to Asia and Africa to take down the warlords who commit genocide. There have been many comparisons of Saddam to Hitler; however, unlike Hitler, who wanted to establish a superior race that would rule the world for a thousand years and who did not care about the total annihilation of a people or his own countrymen to obtain his objective, Saddam cared and knew the limits of evil, even though he massacred the Kurds. Saddam cared enough about being a living legend that he would not commit suicide even though he was held up in a hole and his power had disappeared as quick as dust. And, if you recall, Hitler was so committed to his cause that he committed suicide because he was not going to be humiliated by an inferior force in his mind.

Even though both men were ruthless, they had different mind-sets; one didn't really care about self-preservation or how people viewed him and the other was more concerned about self-preservation.

You don't have to be a political scientist or a high military officer or veteran government person to know that you can't invade a country, remove its leadership, and think you will have the support of all the people. What's sad is that our leadership actually believed Iraqis would be lined up casting flowers at our soldiers as a signal of support and gratitude as soon as we removed Saddam. Over three years later, billions of dollars spent and billions unaccounted for, and over two thousand precious lives lost, we may just be nearing a compromised endstate.

Meanwhile, Osama, who started this mess, has been on the loose producing his tapes of propaganda like 50 cent has been dropping hits. While Osama has been giving us a sample from time to time from his latest album, Iran and North Korea have been busy in the studio producing themselves a guaranteed hit that has already gotten the attention of the world: the nuclear bomb. The next time we think about invading a country and staying, let's be sure we have the will of our people and, more importantly, the will of their people to be gracious hosts. Let's be sure we have several plans and count on the worst scenario. Finally, let's be resolved as a country to do it and finish it right even if we have to mobilize industry or draft personnel.

I don't advocate a cut and run policy; we are too far in this situation to leave. But when I hear the rhetoric from the Republican side that the Democrats want to cut and run, remember that the revered President Reagan cut and ran after the bombing in Beirut.

~It's Good that You Came Out of the Closet, but Don't Think You Own the House~

I think all people should be treated with respect and human dignity. We have laws to protect individual rights, and we should enforce those laws. I personally don't care what your sexual preference is as long as you don't try to make me aware of it; it's akin to someone constantly bragging about themselves or their kids. If you're gay, that's your personal business; if you want to hold your partners' hand or kiss in public, knock yourself out.

However, when there is a movement to legalize marriage between man and man or woman and woman, then that's when I have to say stop. I don't support it because (1) marriage has been declared as a union between man and woman by man's and God's law, more importantly

God's law (2) our society doesn't need the fallout from legitimizing this type of union... we socially accepted single parenthood and now look at the fallout from it. It's ashamed that the gay marriage movement has defined the Democratic Party and taken over the party's agenda. If the party wants to focus on rights, then it should focus on individual rights for all, but not gay marriage. In regard to employment, I definitely don't think a person should be discriminated because of sexual preference.

I initially had a problem with the "don't ask don't tell" policy mandated by the Clinton administration. After that policy was instituted, I along with other officers and noncommissioned Officers thought the military was going to hell in a handbasket. But after really analyzing the matter, I see myself embracing the policy. I've come to see it as "if you're gay, then keep it to yourself." To this day, though, I don't believe homosexuality is compatible with the military, just as it's not compatible with holding a leadership position in the church. I find it quite offensive to know there are ordained gay ministers; it's a slap in the face to God to think that someone with this lifestyle would be leading/teaching others on spiritual matters; it's like leading the blind into a ditch. I know God loves us all, but he laid out his criteria for leadership positions in the church; check out the Book of Timothy.

I know this may be hard for some to swallow, but if you follow the Christianity doctrine, you'll notice that God condemns this lifestyle just as he does the adulterer, drunkard, and others, so why would we want to ignore one over the other? I do believe that a gay person should have rights to visit his or her partner in the hospital and should have rights to personal property if it's bequeathed to him or her. A ratified will by both parties and enforced by the states could rectify this issue. I don't necessarily believe in civil unions. Civil unions bring you one step closer to the traditions and principles of marriage; one could easily make the argument that if you've given me certain privileges, why not give me all? Additionally, many civil union concepts afford partners within a relationship the medical, dental, and other marriage entitlements that would only compound the overstrained systems we now have in place.

The validation of gay marriages further exacerbates the confusion of many young black men, who face probably twice the number of challenges as any other person. As I outlined earlier in the book, the black community is facing a crisis as no other time in history, with single parents outnumbering married couples. Unlike the '40s, '50s, and '60s, there usually is no "village" to raise that child; the burden usually falls on one parent. Many of the young men I've mentored without a male role model in their life are struggling to learn how to be a man. To endorse a lifestyle that is contrary to God and nature only compounds life's hurdles for those young men.

In summary, I detest and protest the gay bashers and will continue to do so. Throughout my life, I've always tried my best to treat people first as human beings, deserving dignity and respect. However, I think spiritual matters are best left up to those that meet God's criteria, and in the case of the military, I think it's best to keep your sexual preference to yourself for the sake of unit cohesion and mission accomplishment.

For the gay advocates who want to compare a gay lifestyle with racial discrimination, I want you to think twice before you use that as an analogy. In my humble opinion, a gay person can wake up one morning or have a revelation and say "I'm gay no more." But ask black men or women to change the color of their skin and see what the outcome is. They will be black tomorrow, the next day, the next week, the next month, and the next year.

~Boy, I Sure Do Hate Paying Them Taxes Every Month~

They say there are two things that are certain in life: death and taxes. To have a functional and democratic style of government, you must have taxes. The burden of protecting our nation, rebuilding after a natural disaster, educating the populace, ensuring we have safe structures and food, and ensuring individual rights are protected rests with a well-funded central government.

No one state can absorb the costs of all these necessities and still be viable and prosperous. I like to think of my tax dollars as money provided to a mutual fund. A mutual fund is a collection of money from a pool of people who provide a share of their earnings in return for an increase in their investment. These people don't all give the same amount; they usually give according to their income. I see the government as the mutual fund and taxes are what the people in the mutual fund provide; they all don't pay the same amount, but do expect a return on their investment. The more you provide (taxes), the more you expect and demand. A mutual fund elects a board to govern/represent its shareholders just as citizens elect its board, Congress. Sometimes the elected board members do an exceptional job managing the funds and sometimes we elect a group that squanders and mismanages the fund, no different from Congress.

I have absolutely no problem paying taxes and paying more incrementally to keep up with inflation or to benefit the people as a whole. I know no group of folks in a state or pool of folks could do all of the things that our government does for us: keep the highways functional, build schools and hospitals, provide protection from criminals, provide public transportation, provide assistance to those in dire straits, and provide relief from natural disasters (this was evident during Hurricane Katrina; well, maybe not Katrina but during many disasters our government has come to the rescue). Therefore, I hate to hear the rhetoric from the Republican Party about slashing taxes and giving back more to the American worker. How much do you think is enough? Five percent, 10 percent, a thousand dollars per year?

I think what they want to say or mean to say is that they want better management of the money; however, slashing taxes resonates with a lot of folks as if they are going to get a whole bunch of money back by siding with the party rhetoric. The real intent of cutting taxes is to stimulate the economy by providing the 5 percent who pay 95 percent of taxes more disposable income, which will in theory encourage them to reinvest, thus creating more jobs. The everyday Joe Blow middle-income and below family won't see the returns in real dollars; however, that family may see price reductions in products and services or even lower interest rates.

In 2006, the Republican-led Congress squeaked through a budget bill to reduce entitlements such as welfare subsidies, cotton subsidies, college subsidies, Medicaid, Medicare, and other programs but still wants to cut taxes for the wealthy... go figure. The 5 percent should reinvest in the American economy anyway, solely because they were blessed to earn it in this country. That's right! Blessed!... without the soldier who is protecting your interest, teachers who educated you, laborers who slaved to ensure you had an environment to be creative, and people who have the free will to purchase your product or service, you wouldn't be where you are today. Wait until one of the tax slash lovers is affected by a natural disaster or his car tire is damaged by a pothole. He or she will be the first one calling for government assistance. We all know taxes are necessary; what I think most Americans want is better management of the taxes they pay.

~Tell Them to Go Home or Tell Them to Stay, but Tell Them Something~

This political issue... this hot potato in my humble opinion... will be the defining moment in American history. If you think that I'm talking about the Iraq War or war on terrorism, you're absolutely wrong. These events are important, but not as important as the issue of immigration. I would say that the issue of immigration today is the first real test of our democracy since civil rights legislation was passed in the 1960s. This issue transcends political parties and has the potential to expose the fairness and decency of the American people.

There are many people in and outside of America who remember Ellis Island and the millions of Europeans who escaped oppression and despondent conditions to be welcome in America with open arms. There are also many people in and outside of America who remember the thousands of Haitians on rafts that were turned away as they tried to escape oppression and despondent conditions.

Now, we as a country are faced with a different scenario: what do we do with the estimated 11 million Mexicans who have crossed the border for a better life? They were not turned away like the Haitians, nor were they fully welcomed like the Europeans. It's a catch-22 situation; in many cases, they provide a valuable resource—labor—and at the same time they can be a drain on local resources such as health care and government subsidies.

What does America do in light of 9/11 and the security of its borders? Can our country absorb the sudden increase in population? How do we secure our borders? What is the process to make the millions of illegal immigrants legal? These are some of the questions that we must deal with to be fair to the immigrants and to the citizens of this country.

The main factor that is preventing us from coming to a fair resolution is fear; fear from the White Anglo-Saxon that he and she will eventually be outnumbered in the years to come by minorities, and fear that political ground and their way of life will be lost. Fear from blacks that their issues will be overlooked by a larger minority group, and fear that the programs designed to overcome discrimination will be spread thin across two races/cultures. Fear from legal immigrants who think their time for citizenship will be prolonged due to the influx of illegal immigrants. These fears, if left to manifest themselves, will eventually turn into hatred and violent acts against those who have crossed the borders to seek a better life. We must have open and honest discussions about this issue and then enact legislation that will fairly address the concerns of all people.

My proposal is to triple the border security and, where necessary, build barriers to prevent the large flow of immigrants into this country. This would reduce the flow of immigrants and deters potential terrorists. Also, I would mandate an identification period, maybe six months to a year, where all illegal immigrants have to register with an agency such as Homeland Security; those who have committed felonies will be immediately deported.

I would also fund and establish assimilation schools, mainly in the heavily populated immigrant areas, and require all immigrants to participate and graduate from this school within the first three years of documentation. These schools will focus on basic English, history of the United States, rights as a citizen, and knowledge and functions of our basic institutions. I would assess a reasonable fine or tax that can be prorated over the course of three years and offer citizenship after six years of demonstrated contribution to society-work.

We must do something, and something soon, or the Klan and many other hate groups will emerge to take control. More importantly, we must do something soon because it is the right thing to do for the American citizen and those who are looking for a better life.

~A Gun, Rifle, Pistol or Firearm for Every Citizen~

Here is another topic that baffles the heck out of me… .gun control. In the United States, there are more guns per capita than in any other country in the world. We have one of the highest violent crime rates of any of the most modern countries on this planet. Keeping those facts in mind, why are there so many objections to gun control? I'm talking about parts of the Brady Bill that dictate a waiting period so that there is "cooling off time" as well as time to conduct a local background check before a gun is sold.

John Hinckley told authorities that if there had been a waiting period, it would have deterred him from purchasing a handgun and shooting President Reagan. The NRA and their advocates go absolutely bananas over the idea of a waiting period and other measures to keep firearms out of the hands of people who don't need them.

Here are some alarming statistics from the Center for Disease, Control and Prevention: a gun in the home is more likely to be used in an attempted suicide than to be used to injure or kill in self-defense; a total of 2,983 young people were killed by firearms in the United States in 2002, including 167 who died in unintentional shootings; when someone was home, a gun was used for protection in fewer than 2 percent of home invasion crimes; and black males accounted for 47 percent of all homicide victims while they only accounted for 6 percent of the population. Vice President Cheney made the unintentional/accidental statistics in February 2006 when he shot a friend while quail hunting. I wonder what he thinks about gun control now?

If you're not a criminal, then you have nothing to worry about. If you think you will one day feel the need to have a firearm to hunt or protect yourself, then go ahead and purchase the firearm before you actually need it… as a matter of fact, if you don't have one right now but are thinking you will need one, then stop reading and go purchase one. If it's so near and dear to your heart, then think of it like an insurance policy; you certainly don't wait until the day that you're in a car wreck to go and purchase car insurance. No! You do it ahead of time. What's up with the folks who want to possess a machine gun? You're certainly not going to hunt with one. Machine guns and rapid-firing weapons are made for one purpose... to kill as many people as possible. They certainly aren't a sports-type weapon, because it takes little skill to spray an area. But if a person believes he or she has the right to own a machine gun or rapid-firing weapon, then he or she should demonstrate the area/range where it will be fired, complete a thorough background check, demonstrate knowledge of the weapon, get finger printed, and recertify the weapon yearly.

What I propose as a compromise is to mandate gun manufacturers to produce weapons with child safety locks or implement out-of-the-box techniques such as weapons with identification methods to prevent anyone other than the owner from firing to reduce theft or illegal transfer, for Congress to ensure we have a waiting period and funding allocated to states to maintain the national data bank for background checks, and for the judicial system to throw out frivolous lawsuits against manufacturers or firearm suppliers who are licensed and comply with the current laws.

I believe law-abiding citizens should have the right to own a firearm and that if we set conditions for usage and ownership and enforce the laws that are already in place we can reduce the crime rate significantly in this country.

~Crime Does Not Pay, So They Say... It All Depends on Who Is Committing the Crime~

I always hear the Republicans stating that we need to be tough on crime. What does that mean? I don't hear much from the Democrats on this issue other than that we need to have a fair and just system. You know, I agree with both.

I believe we should have tough laws for folks who commit violent crimes but at the same time, I would like a justice system to punish equally. Crack cocaine ravaged the black community, and tough laws were put in place and enforced to deal with this epidemic. Many black men and women were given long sentences for possessing or distributing this substance; not many of the users were given a chance to rehabilitate. At the same time, consumption of cocaine didn't taper off; the folks who could afford it continued to use it and distribute it. When the folks who consumed cocaine were caught, they usually received a lighter sentence or were given a chance to rehabilitate. In 1999, the Senate voted to adopt a measure to stiffen the penalty for the sale of powder cocaine, bringing the penalty closer to that given for selling crack cocaine. In my humble opinion, this is an acknowledgment that people of money who usually chose and could afford cocaine were given a much lighter sentence than those who were thrown in jail for crack use or distribution.

A fifteen-year study by the U.S. Sentencing Commission discovered that the 1987 guidelines that placed parameters on judges' sentences had a devastating affect on the black community. Because of these guidelines, the average sentence today is about fifty months, twice what it was before the uniform sentencing system. It's interesting to note that while blacks and whites received an average sentence of slightly more than two years in 1984, blacks stayed in prison for about six years while whites stayed in for about four years.

I saw how the lawmakers handled crack; now I'm curious to see how lawmakers are going to deal with this new epidemic called meth, which has a very devastating affect on families, almost as bad as crack. Meth is a very addictive drug that can be made from household products and over-the-counter drugs. A large percentage of meth production is done in the kitchen. This drug appears to be more appealing to the rural/lower/poorer class of whites, and the effects on this class are similar to what crack did to the inner city/lower/poorer class of blacks. I don't see the coverage that is given to this epidemic and I don't see the same outrage and urging to pass tough laws/sentences against the mothers and fathers who are strung out on meth along with their children. As Fox News says, I want it to be fair and balanced.

White-collar crime to me seems like one of the greatest criminal injustices that we've had over the years. For some reason, most people seem indifferent about this crime and how we handle these criminals. White-collar crime gives one the delusion that the crime is a gentlemen's discretion, a misunderstanding, inaccurate accounting, or something like that. Most people rationalize that they didn't pick up a knife and stab someone to death or in cold blood shoot someone or commit some gruesome crime; you might even think that they didn't hurt anyone. You look at the defendants, who are well groomed, dressed in nice suits, articulate, educated, no criminal record, good standing in the community with functional families, and then you begin to see them as good people who just made a mistake and shouldn't pay that much for just rerouting some money that is transparent to the common person. They certainly shouldn't stay in the same jail as the black, baggy pant, Ebonics talking, uncouth thug who robbed a convenient store with a shotgun. My heavens, these are two totally different people, how in the world could you put them in the same jail?

In my eyes, the criminals like CEO Scott Sullivan of WorldCom, Tyco CEO Dennis Kozlowski, the late Ken Lay and Jeff Skilling of Enron are the worst of them all. They are the wolves who are dressed in sheep's clothing, draining the life of every sheep in their herd. The type of stealing they do or did killed the dreams and future of so many of the hard-working folks within their companies. This type of theft and on that scale is equal to murder in my mind. Think about it, hundreds of decent, hard-working folks were taking a portion of their earnings and reinvesting in the company for a dividend. They were making plans to retire or send their kids to college or pay off their house or to help pay for that needed surgery. Then, greedy, deceitful, cold-blooded, nicely dressed thugs took those funds and spent them at their whim, did crazy accounting to get more money and then tried to hide the fact that the company was having problems all while the workers continued to invest. When these thugs got caught redhanded and the company went under, the retirement funding and any investments disappeared. What didn't disappear were the millions of dollars these thugs stashed away to live off when they return from the jail cottage to their million-dollar estates. They have essentially stolen the lives from these people and should be stripped of their possessions, and given life sentences.

If I were king, they would be in the regular jail, watching their back, I mean butt, at all time like the other inmates. I see disparities just as any other person sees them when it comes to our sentencing laws and the way we look at crime. I know that our political parties can make huge impacts by putting pressure on Congress and the judicial body when it comes to ensuring that we have parity when sentencing and changing the way we look at white-collar crime.

Looking through my lens, I've noticed that the Democrats or liberals have leaned a little too far for the protection of criminals. I do believe there are injustices that occur within the judicial system, but I also know we must be vigilant and diligent to protect law-abiding citizens. I believe we have to be tough on crime and think the following would help (1) If a person is sentenced to five years, then do five years; stop the ridiculous sentencing of thirty years but reducing it to three years for good behavior. Give sentences that merit the crime, and for certain crimes mandatory sentences. (2) Revamp the prison system, rehabilitate those who can be rehabilitated, and let those who can't be trusted in society be. Rehabilitate not coddle; in my mind's eye, rehabilitation is the breakdown and buildup of a person.

I would perform this through a strict regime until the pre-walk stage. From entrance to exit, a dress code, an appearance, an indoctrination of respect for authority and others, and hard work would be the tenants of this program. A typical day would go something like this... early morning wakeup, inspection of room, breakfast, board bus for work project (area beautification), lunch (sack lunch), return to prison, dinner, personal time (one hour), then lights out, six days a week. Once a person completed 85 percent of his or her time and was expected to be paroled, then the remaining time would be spent working and preparing for transition into the world. This would entail job training and classes to emotionally deal with the issues that will be faced on the outside.

~It's Time to Take Away the Cadillac's Parked in Front of the Projects~

Welfare reform as a platform issue was the best thing since sliced bread for the Republican Party. President Reagan galvanized Republicans with several key issues however one resonated well with conservatives, welfare reform. The entitlement days would end by taking the monthly checks away from the lazy folks who were sitting around watching soap operas and driving around in Cadillacs. They would even stop them from selling their food stamps for liquor and weed.

President Reagan really fed the public's fear in times of domestic uncertainty, with images such as an unwed woman with four children driving a Cadillac and parking it in front of her government assistance apartment. During the pre-election debates, Reagan pounced Jimmy Carter on domestic and foreign issues; everyone cheered. Folks who weren't Republicans but identified with his message immediately switched parties and he was elected in a landslide. We never saw welfare reform through the twelve years of Republican reign even though it was a primary platform for each election.

We really didn't see welfare reform until a few courageous governors and state legislatures made changes within their states to reform how they would administer welfare in the early '90s. We didn't see a national plan until a Democrat, President Clinton, signed the Welfare Reform Act in 1996. I truly believe that welfare as it was administered over the past decades did more to the detriment of the poor, especially the black poor. The way it was structured didn't lend itself to creating a two-parent home; it perpetuated a single parent raising a child or children in order to receive subsistence. Although it was designed to be a safety net, it became the only source of income for some generations of families.

The 1996 reform act was intended to provide assistance when needed, but cut the umbilical cord of dependency at some point. It was designed to promote marriage and encourage the formation and maintenance of two-parent families. The main tenet of welfare reform was to assist families by providing job training to become competitive or enter work programs to receive subsistence. The reform or as it is called now, Temporary Assistance for Needy Families (TANF), has helped in some ways to get families out of the welfare cycle. But like any plan, there are areas that need improvement.

I think TANF was long overdue, but would call my version of welfare reform Reduction to Corporate Businesses & Temporary Assistance for Needy Families (RTCB&TANF). If you really want to eliminate entitlements and satisfy the perceptions of many hard-working Americans, then take aim at reducing or eliminating corporate welfare. I think in the Republicans' quest for diversity, this platform would really resonate with blacks and other minorities, so they should try adding this to their campaigns.

Corporate welfare cost taxpayers $87 billion in 2001 compared with roughly $24 billion spent on federal welfare subsidies in 2000. Now, tell me: who are the lazy, trifling, Cadillac-driving, shiftless folks? They are the agribusinesses and executives who wait patiently for their monthly check. The sad thing about these numbers is that agribusinesses and others who receive these handouts have duped or bought off our elected officials with the very same handout. Many people think the local small-time farmer is receiving these subsidies to ensure we maintain a dying craft. But the folks who receive the handouts are the large agribusinesses that grow certain crops such as corn, wheat, soybeans, cotton, and rice. They receive more than 90 percent of all farm subsidies while growers of more than 400 other crops are left out in the cold. The larger farms with those types of crops receive the most while the small farms receive little if nothing to grow their needed crops.

I'm all for welfare reform and was an advocate for reform long before President Clinton signed it into law a decade ago; however, my welfare reform includes corporate as well… as Fox News states, let's keep it fair and balanced.

~Uncle Tom, House Nigger, Boy or Traitor~

I just wanted to take a few lines to address some of the names given to blacks who belong or who have flourished in the Republican Party. It's ironic that only a few decades ago whites who supported equal rights for blacks or those who went out of their way to help blacks were called "nigger lovers" or some other derogatory term. Now you have blacks who are essentially doing it to their own by calling other blacks who have a different viewpoint white lovers.

For some reason, many blacks feel betrayed because

a few blacks have a different view on how to get to the Promised Land and for some strange reason, feel that they are less black because they reason or think differently. Some black Democrats might say that they don't agree with everything the Democratic Party stands for, but that it is closer to their viewpoints than the Republican Party. I respect that and I also respect the brother or sister who believes that the Republican Party is the closest to his or her stand on their issues. What I don't respect is the name-calling or the inferences that because a black person is a Republican, then he or she is less black or a traitor.

I have black Republican friends/acquaintances and can tell you that they are just as black as some of my Democrat friends; as a matter of fact, some of them had rougher times than the average black Democrat. It's all about respect and self-confidence to have an open mind and listen to varying viewpoints; I think some of our so-called leaders need a dose of open-mindness. Folks like Secretary of State Rice, retired General Colin Powell, and Congressman J. C. Watts have done great things for blacks and all Americans; however, you won't hear much about their contributions because the so-called black leadership and black media want you to think they are traitors or less than black.

I've never met any of these giants, but have read about them or talked with others who know them. They all came from very tough backgrounds, were discriminated against, reached down to help someone, and still managed to achieve great military and political feats. I've read Colin

Powell's and J. C. Watts' autobiographies and was inspired by both men. Those who call them derogatory names or think they are less than black, do some research yourself to come up with your own conclusion. You might be surprised to learn that some of the very same folks who call them names haven't done a tenth of the things these folks have done for the black community. Don't follow the party line; inform yourself and make up your own mind.

~Understanding the Parties~

The two major political parties have recently been unfairly defined by extremists within their camps. The extremists' personal quests have become a symbol of what I think most Americans hate. They have set the agenda for their respective party, supplied the funding to advertise their case, and expect elected officials within the party to back them. They are so obsessed with their issues that they think most Americans agree or think as they do. If they realize that the majority of Americans don't support their idea, then they shrug it off and rationalize that the majority are clueless and that they know what's best because they either have superior intellectual ability or have a higher calling that only a few understand. It's like a disease that has spread over the last few years from the extremists to their party's congressmen; it has infected some congressmen on both sides of the aisle.

It is part of the reason why we have such a divisive Congress and also part of the reason why people have taken sides as if they were enemies. The corruption, the scandals, and constant fighting among parties have put a nasty taste in the mouths of the American public, and there are rumblings from supporters of both parties to purge the diseased congressmen from their parties. Although I don't agree with everything former Governor and Senator Zell Miller espouses on the problems with the Democratic Party, he does address a need to move more to the center. From my viewpoint, I think there needs to be a purging of the whining, complaining, moaning, and bitching from Democratic Party leadership. One thing that I can't stand is for someone to bring to my attention an issue without proposing a solution to the problem; I'm thick skinned but can't stand a complainer.

Whether it's the nomination of Roberts or Alito, the Patriot Act, or even the Iraq War, it's difficult to understand why the party is against an issue other than it's against the nomination, the act, or war.

The Republican Party has its issues as well, and former Republican Senator and diplomat Danforth wants his party to tone down the religious rhetoric and focus on issues central to all Americans. From my viewpoint, I think there needs to be a purging of the arrogance, stubbornness, and holier than thou mentality within the Republican Party. Although the party has controlled Congress over the last decade or so, it won't last for long if it continues to try to force its beliefs on people without acknowledging mistakes made. The party leadership is eloquently informing the public that it has been fiscally responsible, the war is going just the way they expected, there is no corruption within the party, you're unpatriotic if you disagree with the war, and if you're a Democrat you are destined to hell, to name a few.

American citizens want healthy debates and want to know that their representative is passionate about his or her duty, but certainly doesn't want nor expect the type of cutthroat politics we've witnessed over the past few years.

Chapter VIII

Who's Got Ya Back?

"The true measure of a man is how he treats someone who can do him absolutely no good." - Samuel Johnson (1709-1784)

I KNOW MY immediate family members want the very best for me, are concerned about me, and will do everything possible to protect my interests... they have my back. I also know that they have limited powers to protect me and I them; however, we all know that we have a higher power who has all of our backs. We also know that he has given man certain abilities, intelligence, and reason to use that power as he sees fit, he can use it wisely or unwisely.

I can use my God-given talents and power to help my family and friends, but that might not be enough to protect them from all the things they will face in life. As a result, I have to expect that there is an earthly entity or being that has power given to him or her through a collective body of folks such as me to look out for the interests of people. This entity could be the government, local officials, designated leaders, law enforcement agents, community-based organizations, church leaders, and others. I would say that some of these entities and folks have my back as well.

Most of these organizations and people derive their power from everyday folks who fund, support, and consent to allow these groups or folks to represent them and their family. Some of these organizations and people excel in keeping their end of the bargain. One such entity is the government and it has gotten better in protecting the interests of its citizens but had a relapse after Hurricane Katrina hit the Gulf Coast and its interpretation of the eminent domain law. The government has allowed self-interest groups to take property away from average, hard-working citizens in the name of new malls, casinos, and commercial developments. Many of these governmental acquisitions were not necessary for the betterment of the populace but for the betterment of the government's bank account. As a result, these individuals were betrayed by the very same organization that is supposed to have their backs, the same organization that they funded and supported.

The local, state, and federal governments' response to Hurricane Katrina was atrocious, to say the least. The richest and most powerful country in the world couldn't take care of its displaced citizens and early in 2006 was still struggling to get basic necessities to the folks in the Gulf Coast.

If I were president, I would hire Oprah to disperse

the money and ensure that government funds were spent properly; she has done more proportionately with the approximately $10 million of her own that was used to build houses and communities than the government has done with its many billions. That's the government, and we can cite instance after instance where some folks thought the government had their back only to be betrayed. What about the organizations that are supposed to have the backs of blacks and other minorities such as the National Association for the advancement of Colored People (NAACP), the Urban League, black Greek fraternities, the Brotherhood of Sleeping Car Porters (BSCP), the National Council for Negro Women, the Southern Christian Leadership Conference (SCLC), and other types of organizations? I mentioned some of these because many of these organizations have deep history and have had a profound affect and impact on the lives of blacks.

The NAACP, founded by whites and blacks, was the icon of the civil rights movement. This organization championed many discrimination cases, brought to light injustices, and organized legal fights or protests to deal with the plight of blacks and minorities.

Black Greek organizations were founded by visionary men and women at predominately white universities to network and assist each other. These fraternal organizations are now international with hundreds of thousands of members, many of whom have broken racial and gender barriers to become great leaders of America.

The National Urban League got its start in the early 1900s by helping blacks who migrated from the South transition into an urban environment. This organization was relevant through the civil rights era as it assisted blacks in obtaining educational and vocational training and placement.

The National Negro Council for Women was born in the 1930's to promote the well being of African American women and their families. This council effectively brought together women's coalitions and groups to maximize the effect and impact of their message.

The SCLC was born in the late 1950s as a coalition of activists, religious leaders, and community leaders to unite regardless of religious affiliation to fight racism. Dr. Martin Luther King Jr. was the founding president, and many SCLC members were or became mediators for white and black issues.

The BSCP consisted of a group of black servants on trains who organized themselves into the first black union and essentially planted the seed for the civil rights movement. These great men, led by A. Phillip Randolf, were truly the new underground railroad of information as they would collect newspapers from various cities and share their experiences with blacks in the South and North.

The aforementioned organizations were all led by passionate men and women who felt it necessary to protect the interests of blacks during times of racism and inequality. These organizations were born at the right time and filled a protection gap that was left void by local, state, and federal governments.

In some cases, organizations such as the BSCP and SCLC lost their relevance as the black movement progressed and times changed. The NAACP, National Negro Council of Women, black Greek organizations, and the Urban League have endured the test of time and are still performing their mission. Are their tactics and strategies to watch my back or your back still relevant? I have no doubt that these organizations want to do their best, but I think they are off-balance with their direction and focus. In my humble opinion, there are too many marches, too many social events, too many meaningless summits, and not enough action to deal with the issues that affect us. We still need these organizations, but need their collective power to focus on strategies to deal with homelessness, single parenting, making men of deadbeat dads, economic empowerment, small business assistance, community development, moral direction and backbone, educational opportunities through mentorship, and scholarships, to name a few. As Phillip Randolf became frustrated with the black leaders who were part of the old crowd during the early 1900s, I and I'm sure other blacks are displeased with the direction of some of our historic organizations. You see, many of us have given our support and funding to these organizations to watch our backs; we're just not sure they have our backs totally covered.

~Heroes~

When you think of heroes, you may think of some fictional character such as Superman or Batman. Or, you may think of Harriet Tubman, the leader of the Underground Railroad who never lost a runaway slave, or you may think of Benjamin Banneker, a self-taught astronomer who published the almanac and who some say was the designer of Washington, D.C. Or you may think of Marian Anderson, a renowned opera singer and first black to be a permanent member of the Metropolitan Opera Company, as well as the first to perform at the White House. Or you may think of track star Jesse Owens, who won four medals during the Olympics and dismissed Hitler's racial superiority assertion. Or you may think of George Washington Carver, who devised hundreds of uses for the peanut and was known internationally as a great scientist/researcher. Or you may think of Medgar Evers, the NAACP field secretary in Mississippi who gave his life to an assassin for helping blacks. Or you may think of Thurgood Marshall, who was instrumental in striking down separate but equal laws and later became the first black to sit on the Supreme Court.

All of these individuals and many other famous blacks had the backs of other blacks and were looking out for their best interests. Some of them withstood threats to themselves and families and some were even assassinated, but all chose to accept the power given to them by other blacks and minorities to represent them and cover their back. These individuals knew their talents and wanted to use them to break down barriers or help someone else.

Some say a hero is a lucky person who happens to be at the right place at the right time and in the face of fear overcomes that fear to sacrifice his personal safety or well-being for the sake of others. They even say that you don't have to be smart or necessarily fit to be a hero; just meet the criteria above and you're labeled as a hero for life. In my book, you don't have to be the first, the lucky one, or famous to be a hero. All you have to do is to maximize your God-given talents to help yourself and, more importantly, to help someone else, which leads me to the everyday heroes.

The everyday heroes are the mothers and fathers who raise their children in a loving home, educate them, spiritually feed them, discipline them, and release them when it's time. These heroes are my parents, and possibly your parents, who didn't receive awards, positions of authority, medals, or recognition by dignitaries for their hard work. They received the occasional "thank you" or "I love you" on special occasions such as Mother's Day or Father's Day.

The everyday heroes are also the public servants such as policemen, firemen, and soldiers who put their life on the line every day to protect your back and my back. These folks didn't sign up for this type of career to become famous; as a matter of fact, some of them are despised by the very same people they protect. They certainly didn't sign up for the pay or the glory, and you only hear about the heroic things they do when there is a conflict. All of the sacrifices they make, all of the long hours they dedicate to their work, and all of the inhumane things they witness should make everyone of them a hero each and every day. However, we only recognize them when they save a child from a burning house, engage our enemies in combat, or stop a crime. In my book, these folks are my supermen and superwomen.

~Unsung Heroes~

We all hear about the public figures who donate money and give their time to make dreams come true for everyday folks. They include Oprah Winfrey, who donates money to HBCUs and other various charities; Tom Joyner, who raises and donates money to HBCUs and deserving single parents; Magic Johnson who enhances the poor communities with Starbucks or his Magic Johnson theaters; football star Warrick Dunn who is committed to helping single mothers by purchasing houses for them; or Jim Brown, who established Amer-I-Can organization that promotes anti-drug use for youth. But what about the everyday folks who do hero-type work in their community and don't receive the recognition they so richly deserve?

You know the folks I'm talking about, those who quietly and inconspicuously donate their time and money to help others. You never see these folks bragging about how much they donated to a cause, nor do you see them advertise the time they spent volunteering to help a cause. Many of these folks go through life doing more than their fair share of work helping others and you may hear about them locally, but definitely won't hear about them regionally or nationally. They might get lucky and be honored with the naming of a street or community center after them or receive some type of recognition during church service.

In my mind, they are doing God's work and are akin to the widow who gave her one penny or mite, all that she had, during worship. I have the most admiration for these folks because they use one or two God-given talents and allow him to multiply it by hundreds for his benefit. In my book, these are the unsung heroes. They are folks like my mom who gives her time and money to charity and who people call on during times of distress for comfort. She is well known in her community and in my mind has celebrity like status. No matter where she goes, to the mall, doctor's office, restaurant, sports outing, or church, there is always someone who approaches her and tells her thanks for the words of advice or for the financial help or for volunteering at an event. It's nothing unusual to go to her house and see a couple staying in the house while they get on their feet or see South Africans from her church exchange program staying in her house. I sometimes have to check with my mother before I come home to see if she has room to accommodate my family and me.

She didn't just start helping folks when I left the house over twenty years ago; she did it when I was there and in her words will do it until she is taken away from this earth.

Unsung heroes include Charles Drugger of Baltimore, Maryland, who is a school teacher and revolutionary type person but possesses a passion unmatched in his willingness to help inner city youth. Charles sometimes takes fifteen to twenty inner-city youth camping and swimming at his expense and exposes them to various cultural events. He organizes an annual swim splash party to offset his Camp Harambee, parade and other events that he sponsors.

Charles's wife didn't understand why he spent so much time and so much of their money helping young boys and girls who weren't related to them, but after doing some soul searching, she came to peace and now understands and supports his activities. You will never hear him boast about what he does; he just does it and keeps on driving on.

My good friend Tony Harrison of Woodbridge, Virginia, who helps me out with the mentorship program is an unsung hero. Tony is a single brother with no kids of his own. He finds the time in his hectic schedule to mentor, teach, organize and haul kids to the movies, the football games, the museum, or wherever we go for a cultural outing. Tony is also in charge of our one-week-long, free of charge, overnight summer camp that accommodates up to fifty young boys. He is responsible for all aspects of the camp, which costs our fraternity approximately $30,000 to run and is staffed solely by volunteers. Tony is a reliable and dedicated brother who is definitely a hero in my book.

Another unsung hero is Phyllis Poller of Waycross, Georgia, a high school math teacher, devoted mother, and unofficial educational counselor. Phyllis has an unrelenting passion for education and will see to it that any young man or woman who has a desire or has the potential for a secondary education gets into college. Almost all of the people she helps are the first in their family to attend college, and many of their parents just don't have the means or access to get them in college. Phyllis barrels through the bureaucracy, finds the appropriate loans/grants, gets the documents, assists in filling them out, helps the parents pay initial fees, and take the parents and young men or women to visit the campus at her expense. Phyllis has made personal sacrifices to see to it that her children, as she states, get that paper so they can be successful in life. All the young men and women she has helped could be assembled and you would have enough to dress out two basketball squads.

Another unsung hero is Oseola McCarty of Hattiesburg, Mississippi, who grew up in the early 1900s and worked backbreaking jobs to earn a living. She cooked for the elite in Mississippi and later did laundry to earn money. Oseola lived a frugal life, not making much money but putting away a few cents each time from her earnings. She never had a car, always walked to her destinations, and had to be persuaded to purchase a window air conditioner for her sixty-year-old house. Ms. McCarty also had a passion for education and understood the necessity of such. At age eighty-seven, she donated $150,000 to Southern

Mississippi University. The money was used for the Oseola McCarty Scholarship, with priority given to deserving African Americans enrolling in the university.

Another unsung hero is retired Colonel Walter McCreary of Springfield, Virginia, one of the original Tuskegee Airmen who went through hell to prove other folks wrong about the intellectual abilities of blacks. Walter has a passion for youth and wants all to succeed given the many opportunities now available that he and others did not have. Although in his eighties, Walter is always willing to share his experiences with young men and women or anyone who will listen to his experiences and advice.

Another unsung hero is Deborah Thomas of Washington, D.C., who turned her life around from drugs to become a leader in her community. Deborah was elected as the tenant association president for a dilapidated building that was home for many poor hard-working minority families. Amid the gentrification in D.C., Deborah with the help of benevolent black financers and attorneys led the tenants in a four-year, life-changing journey to purchase their newly renovated apartments. This was a feat in itself because the property they lived in was one of the most sought-after properties in the District. With the help of others, she led a group of families whose average income was just over $20,000 per year to make a $12 million purchase and rehabilitation of the property. Deborah wasn't a fame seeker; she believed that everyone had a right to own their own house no matter if they were poor blacks and Hispanics.

I'm sure you know or can think of some unsung heroes. Please tell them how much they are appreciated; they too need to know that we are grateful that they have our backs.

Chapter IX

Things that make you go HMMM!!!

"I have always thought the actions of men the best interpreters of their thoughts." –John Locke

O. J. vs. Robert Blake

WHY WAS O. J.'s trial the trial of the century? Was it because a black celebrity allegedly murdered his white wife and friend? Why was there such a division amongst blacks and whites on his innocence before the trial began? Why did blacks erupt in cheers and whites in tears during the reading of his verdict? Could it be that some folks thought that he was automatically guilty because he was black and that the circumstantial evidence sufficed? Or did some people feel that he did commit the crime but because he had money and celebrity status he got off? Or did some feel that the verdict was a repayment for the many innocent blacks who were wrongfully accused and executed in the past?

I don't know who felt what, but why in the heck didn't we raise the same commotion about Robert Blake who allegedly killed his wife in cold blood outside a café?

Violence in Hockey

Why are hockey players allowed to fight during their games? Why do they fight almost every night? During the fight, why do referees stand off to the side and allow the players to duke it out until a winner is determined? Why do NBA and NFL players who get in a scuffle, not even a fight, get branded as thugs and not the hockey players? Why were people so outraged when Ron Artest leaped into the stands to hit a fan who he thought threw a drink on him, yet there was half the coverage and outrage from people when a hockey player took a cheap shot at another player that nearly cost him his life?

The Word "Nigger"

Why do some black folks call other black folks "Nigger" in public? Why do some black rappers, actors and comedians use the word "Nigger" in their acts or music if they think it is offensive if someone outside of their race calls them that? Why do some black folks get pissed off when other races refer to blacks as Niggers?

Rapper Questions

Why did Kaye West state that we need to have a moratorium against gay bashing when he endorses music that calls women "bitches and ho's"? Why do most black rappers think they speak for all blacks? Why do some rappers have so much plaque (gold covers) on their teeth? With the money they make, don't they know they can have their teeth cleaned to make them shiny ivory white? Why do most rappers always talk about shootin' someone, sexin' someone, drinkin' something, smokin' something, or ridin' something... Do rappers know there is much more to life than doing all them somethings?

Oscar Awards

Out of all the wonderful and insightful movies that Denzel Washington and Halle Berry starred in, why did they win an Oscar for the most degrading and out-of-character movie they ever starred in? Why didn't Halle win an Oscar for *Dorothy Dandridge* and Denzel for *Glory* or *Hurricane*?

PETA Folks

Why do PETA folks think that killing a fish is cruel? Why do some folks want to take their personal views to the extreme and then try to force them on everyone else? Why do you think the PETA rep who was on Fox News state that the group's analysis had determined that a fish has feelings and when caught on a hook that it causes cruel and unusual pain? Do you think I'm going to stop eating catfish? Better yet, do you think if I catch a catfish, clean him real quick, fry him up real quick, and eat him real quick that it won't hurt him as much? Why was the PETA rep on Fox wearing a leather belt and leather shoes?

I wonder if he asked the cow if he could borrow some skin to make his belt and shoes?

Gas Prices

Why did the gas prices go up astronomically during hurricanes Wilma, Rita, and Katrina? Why did the oil executives state that they did not price-gouge folks in America when they realized record earnings during those months? If we can send a man to the moon and back or develop a micro chip the size of a fingernail that can store volumes of material, then how come we can't develop an alternative fuel source that is affordable, plentiful, and environmentally safe? If someone developed such a fuel source, how many days, no, how many hours would they stay alive? How did the advocates of natural gas fool us to believe that natural gas is cheaper than electricity?

Fads

Why do some young men wear their pants hanging off their butts? Why don't they get a belt to hold them up instead of using their thumb to hold them up? When they walk, why do they waddle like they just had a bowel movement in their pants? I wonder if they know that if they continue to waddle like that, then they could possibly change the bone structure in their legs and it would be permanent. Why do some young men and women leave their boots or sneakers untied? Do you think they know that is the number one cause of tripping?

White Flight

Why do some white folks flee a neighborhood once blacks or other minorities begin to move in? Don't they know that the same blacks who moved in their neighborhood would follow them to the moon if they established a neighborhood on it and the transportation costs were within reason?

Weight-loss Schemes

Why do they show a sculptured person on TV before and after they have used a weight-lifting device or weight-reduction product? Why do many of them advertise that you can see these same results in six or twelve weeks? Don't they know that it takes more than those machines or pills or drink and much more time to get in that kind of shape?

Homeless Folks

Why are there so many homeless people in the nation's capital? Do you receive extra benefits for being homeless in the capital? Why don't you see homeless folks or a shelter in a small or rural town?

Music

Why do some high school and big college bands insist on playing the theme from *Star Wars* or a classical song or some song from the 1920s during halftime? Don't they know that's why people leave during halftime, except for the parents of the kids and the folks from the 1920s?

Isn't it funny to be in a parking lot and hear a loud, thumping, raucous rap song and automatically think it is a black kid in the car and you look over and see a bunch of preppy white kids in a mustang bopping their heads to music? Isn't that funny? It is to me.

Gansta Rappers Commercialized

I always thought that the Gansta Rappers were to keep it real and live the life they portray in their music. So, if they make money off of their records, then they should not move into the elite neighborhoods but remain in the hood to help others, right? That would be keeping it real, right? Maybe I'm wrong, but I thought that you become a sellout if you go mainstream with corny commercials and TV shows? Nothing against Ice T but didn't he make a song about killing a cop and even though its about a rogue cop, several years later he made big cheddar for portraying a cop on *Law and Order*. I wonder if he is worried that someone might shoot him now that he portrays a cop on TV?

National Black Anthem

Why is "Lift Every Voice and Sing" labeled as the national black anthem? I thought the national anthem was the "Star-Spangled Banner"; no one ever told me that there was a black anthem. Is there a national black flag that I'm supposed to salute or come to attention when the national black anthem is played? I'm proud to be black and just as proud to be an American, but would like to think that I believe in the spirit of inclusiveness, that's what the civil rights leaders and others fought for. Therefore, I think I will honor the "Star-Spangled Banner" as the national anthem and respect Lift Every Voice and Sing" as a powerful song but not my anthem.

Confederate Flag

Why after 150 years and a devastating loss by the South do some folks insist on flying the Confederate flag on a public building? If they fly that symbol of racial divisiveness and everything that this country is against on their private property, then I really don't care, but why cant they adapt to change just as millions of blacks and other minorities had to do during times of oppression?

Family Reunions

Are black people the only ones who have family reunions? Why don't you see whites, Asians, or Hispanics gathered at a park or resort area during the summer or Labor Day with a red, white, blue, green, yellow, brown, or even purple shirt on that reads 'The Browns, Smiths and Jones, 25th Annual Family Reunion, Orlando, Florida"?

Hair

Why do some males who are going bald swirl their hair from the back of their neck or from the side to cover the area that is going bald, the way Donald Trump does? Don't they know that they draw more attention to their baldness? Why do some women place yellow, red, or purple extensions in their hair? Do they really... I mean do they really, want to draw attention to themselves? What if gerry curls came back in style? Would you get a gerry curl if you had a cloth material sofa? Do you know that there are some true OPs (original players) who were never told that gerry curls went out of style two decades ago? I've seen them.

Technology

For the technically challenged people like me, can they slow down the pace at which an item becomes obsolete? I had just gotten used to the shoulder-carrying VCR with the bright light when they introduced the handheld version. I'm comfortable with the shoulder-carrying kind and know it inside and out, but do you think people will laugh or stare at me if I record one my children's game with it? What was wrong with the VCR movies? DVDs are OK but again for the technically challenged, why did they cover up half the movie screen with a widescreen version when they know that I and many others have the picture tube TV and just can afford the flat screen plasma TV?

Five-Star Restaurants

Who determines the criteria for a five-star restaurant? Why do five-star restaurants serve you bread such as olive bread that most people don't eat? Why do they list all that stuff on the menu that you've never heard of? Who told them that frog legs, snails, or sheep's head soup was a delicacy? Why do they spend all of their time decorating a plate and accenting the food with green flowery stuff you've never heard of? How come they can't serve hot, buttery bread the way Golden Corral does? Why don't they spend less time decorating and more time filling the plate with edible food? Why don't they list items on the menu that everyone knows and understands like chicken, fried that is, green beans, mashed potatoes, and peach cobbler? I know what you are thinking: I can give it a fancy name like submerged domestic feathery fowl (that would be fried chicken), soufflé tatos with a hint of pasteurized sauce (that would be mashed potatoes with butter), delightful garden stalks seasoned with an array of colorful enhancers (that would be green beans with salt and pepper). To top your meal, we would have heavenly layers of forbidden fruit tamed with a spicy crust within and on top (you got it, peach cobbler).

Service

Why do some people who work in the service industry look and act as if you are inconveniencing them when you ask for help or order from them? Why do they sigh, slump their shoulders, talk loud, or even get an attitude when you ask them a legitimate question? Shouldn't they be ecstatic and jumping for joy if you are helping to pay their salary?

Business Practices

Why does the phone, cable, utility, or gas company

harass you if you are late with your payment? Especially, if you've had service for years and always paid on time. Why do they send those threatening letters or call you at work to make you feel bad? When they owe you for an overcharge, why do you have to find out yourself that they made a mistake opposed to them harassing you with apology letters and phone calls? When they owe you, why do they wait until the next month to refund your money and when you owe them, why do they want it right away?

Tipping

Who came up with the 15 percent rule for tipping? Why not 10 percent or 5 percent or whatever you want to leave? For the businesses whose workers only receive tips for wages, how come they don't advertise in the paper or phone book or put a disclaimer on the front door stating that their workers work for tips only? If they did that, then I could make up my mind if I want to pay for someone to prepare my food and then pay for someone to bring it out to my table. How come they don't include the tip in the price of the meal? Wouldn't that make things a lot easier? It would to me.

Summary

"How far you go in life depends on your being tender with the young, compassionate with the aged, sympathetic with the striving and tolerant of the weak and strong. Because someday in your life you will have been all of these." George Washington Carver

AS THE DEACON SAYS, "I hope something I said was beneficial and edifying for you." I truly hope that I pricked your mind and may have reinforced or given you some ideas on how to make the black community and our world better.

From my humble beginnings to my experiences and observations of the black church to the challenges we face in the sports realm to the importance of education to viewing the black community through a critical lens to balancing our checkbooks to voting with our eyes open to identifying the real heroes to making you wonder why, I wanted this to be an interesting and thought-provoking read. I know that I may have stated something that you disagree with, and that's OK. If you disagree, then more than likely you will research or observe to prove me wrong. If your research or observations prove me wrong, then I'm thankful that you took time to find the answer for yourself as opposed to believing everything you hear and read. If your research proves me right, then that's OK as well. If you are indifferent to the content of this book, then I apologize, but please tell someone else about the book.

Remember, the content of this book is about my humble opinions, viewpoints, and observations, occasionally supported by statistics. We all look at life through different lenses; sometimes we are focused on the same things and sometimes we aren't and sometimes we need to calibrate our lens so that we are in harmony with each other. Hopefully, I didn't rain on your parade but provide a rainbow of thoughts that might inspire you. Again, thank you and did I tell I you I was blessed?

Acknowledgments

MY MOM ALWAYS told me that I needed to stay in contact with folks because you never know who will be there for you in times of need. She stressed the importance of reaching out to relatives and friends and de-emphasized taking the alone approach to life. She was right, however, when you are young, healthy and feel invincible then you tend to think that you've accomplished everything by yourself; you somehow forget about your support system and the contributions they made to your development. I want to publicly thank the folks who have shaped and molded me as well as the folks who have contributed to the content of this book.

I first want to give thanks to the higher power we call God, Allah, Jehovah, and other wonderful names; for it not for him we would not be where we are today. I want to thank my most important support system, my family and that includes uncles, aunts, grandparents, in laws and cousins. I want to personally thank the woman who has been in my life almost half of my life; my wife, Lisa. She is truly the better half and I definitely wouldn't have made it as far as I did in my career or accomplished the many goals in life without her.

I want to thank my mother, Pat Horton, who has always been there for me and is the role model that I want my wonderful daughter to emulate. To my father who is not here but know that he is overlooking me, thanks for being a responsible and consistent man in my life.

To our children, Aaron and Ashley, I'm proud of you both and couldn't have been blessed with better children.

I also want to extend my thanks to my in-laws who took me in as an immediate family member without hesitation, especially my mother in-law, Lena Poller.

Now, for the folks who have been real contributors of this book, my hat goes off to my sounding board, coffee and lunch buddy, Wilson Russ. I also want to thank those who provided insight or connected me with other folks who helped formulate my thoughts; Tyrone Brumfield, Dexter Davis, Sybil Dunegan, Miya Fennar, Ed Naylor, and Cathy Simmons...thanks. I want to thank the Alexandria-Fairfax chapter of Kappa Alpha Psi who gave me the privilege of working with some great young men.

Additionally, I want to acknowledge this chapter for being one of the most involved and influential chapters in the Country. I would be remiss if I didn't thank graphic artist and fraternity brother, Tony Baker, who gave me the idea for the cover. Thanks to my editor, Melanie Rigney, for her insight and word smoothing. Lastly, thanks to all my friends and acquaintances in the military, in D.C., Atlanta, and around the world.

Bibliography

Gaul, Gilbert M., and Frank Fitzpatrick. "The rise of the major college athletic empires," Knight-Ridder Newspapers, September 27, 2000.

Greene, Stuart, April Lidinsky, and Kevin Gibley, eds. *Constructing Identities: A Rhetoric and Reader.* Needham Heights, MA: Pearson, 1999.

Grusky, David B., ed. *Class, Gender, Race: Social Stratification in Sociological Perspective*, 2nd ed. Boulder, CO: Westview Press, 2001.

Guthrie, James W., et al. *Schools and Inequality.* Cambridge, MA: MIT Press, 1971, quoted at http://www.nd.edu/~mtardy/JDonnelly.html.

Hanushek, Eric. "The Impact of Differential Expenditures on Student Performance." *Educational Researcher* 18, no. 4 (May 1989): 45-51, quoted at http://eric.uoregon.edu/publications/digests/digest119.html.

Harp, Lonnie. "Dollars and Sense: Reformers Seek To Rethink School Financing To Make It a Powerful Lever of Change." *Education Week* 12, no. 27 (March 31, 1993a): 9-14, quoted at http://eric.uoregon.edu/publications/digests/digest083.html.

Hirsch, E. D. "What Every American Needs to Know," quoted at http://www.nd.edu/~mtardy/JDonnelly.html.

Kozol, Jonathan. "Other People's Children: North Lawndale and the South Side of Chicago," quoted at http://www.nd.edu/~mtardy/JDonnelly.html.

—"Excerpts from the book *Savage Inequalities: Life on the Mississippi: East St. Louis, Illinois.*" Quoted at http://www.nd.edu/~mtardy/JDonnelly.html.

Slivinski, Stephen. "The corporate welfare budget bigger than ever." *Policy Analysis* 415. Walsh, Joan. "How some inner cities are funding pathways out of misery," *Jinn* 2.25 (December 2-December 15, 1996).

Wilson, William Julius. "Jobless Poverty: A New Form of Social Dislocation in the Inner-City Ghetto." In *A Nation Divided: Diversity, Inequality, and Community in American Society,* Phyllis Moen, Donna Dempster-McClain, and Henry Walker, eds. Ithaca, NY: Cornell University Press, 1998.

—*The Truly Disadvantaged: The Inner City, the Underclass, and Public Policy.* Chicago: The University of Chicago Press, 1987.